PRAYING IS POWERFUL

Organised Christian Prayers To Ask God For Help For Yourself & Your Loved Ones

Selva Sugunendran

CEng, MIEE, MCMI, CHt, MIMDHA, MBBNLP, MABNLP
#1 Best Selling Author, Speaker & Coach

Copyright © 2021 by Selva Sugunendran: BlessMeLord.com

ISBN: 9798451193334

All rights reserved. No part of this book may be reproduced or transmitted in any form or by any means, electronic or mechanical, including photocopying, recording, or by any information storage and retrieval system, without permission in writing from the Copyright owner.

Medical Disclaimer: The author of this book is a competent, experienced writer. He has taken every opportunity to ensure all information presented here is correct and up to date at the time of writing. No documentation within this book has been evaluated by the Food and Drug Administration, and no documentation should be used to diagnose, treat, cure, or prevent any disease.

Any information is to be used for educational and information purposes only. It should never be substituted for the medical advice from your own doctor or other health care professionals.

We do not dispense medical advice, prescribed drugs or diagnose any illnesses with our literature.

The author and publisher are not responsible or liable for any self or third-party diagnosis made by visitors based upon the content in this book. The author or publisher does not in any way endorse any commercial products or services linked from other websites to this book.

Please consult your doctor or health care specialist if you are in any way concerned about your physical wellbeing.

Table Of Contents

FOREWORD..vi

DEDICATION..x

ABOUT THE AUTHOR xi

ACKNOWLEDGEMENT xiv

AUTHOR'S NOTE: xvi

THE BOOK OF 250 PRAYERS xix

Chapter 1: PRAYER OF THANKSGIVING 1

Chapter 2: PRAYER FOR OVERCOMING TRIALS 24

Chapter 3: PRAYERS TO OVERCOME WRONG HABITS............... 55

Chapter 4: PRAYERS TO GROWING IN THE WORD 77

Chapter 5: PRAYER FOR DIVINE HEALING 109

Chapter 6: PRAYER FOR PROSPERITY & BUSINESSES 137

Chapter 7: PRAYER FOR CHRISTIAN LIVING............................. 166

Chapter 8: PRAYER FOR THE LOVE OF GOD............................. 209

Chapter 9: PRAYING FOR YOUR FAMILY 231

Chapter 10: PRAYER TO ENJOY YOUR INHERITANCE IN CHRIST 244

Chapter 11: PRAYER FOR YOUR NATION................... 257

Chapter 12: PRAYER FOR GOD'S GRACE................... 270

ALL BOOKS PUBLISHED BY AUTHOR OF THIS BOOK 278

BOOKS ON CREATION & EVOLUTION 279

BOOKS ON WELLNESS & HEALTH 280

BOOKS ON ALZHEIMER'S & DEMENTIA 281

BOOKS ON SUCCESS 282

BOOK ON AUTISM & ASPERGER'S SYNDROME 283

BOOKS ON CHRISTIAN BELIEFS: 284

FOREWORD

There are many ways in which God influences us and helps us through turmoil, and praying is one of the best ways to get closer to Him.

God delights in the prayers of the saints and wants us to pray to Him. As He invites us to pray, He's always willing and excited to answer our prayers.

He knows what you want to pray about before you even start praying, yet He still invites you, as prayer is more than just asking for things. Prayer is a fellowship, a communion and drinking together from the same cup.

There is a God-prescribed way to pray, which will allow you to receive answers to your prayers and for your prayers to be effective.

The Word of God says the sacrifice (Prayer) of sinners is an abomination to God "The sacrifice of the wicked is an abomination to the Lord, but the prayer of the upright is his delight" Proverbs 15:8. So when your prayer ultimately ascends to God, and you receive answers, it is a privilege that you must not take lightly.

The Spirit of God has been uniquely designed to provide you with an awesome opportunity to not only pray for yourself but for others. It includes a platform, which will enable you to intercede for other people to help them change their states and situations.

The fact that you've found this book is not by chance but because God has orchestrated it. He wants to help you improve your life and others around you… "And I sought for a man among them that should make up the hedge and stand in the gap before me for the land, that I should not destroy it: but I found more" Ezekiel 22:30.

In this book, you will explore a myriad of themes in prayer, such as:

Thanksgiving, Overcoming Trials, Overcoming Wrong Habits, Growing in the Word, Prosperity/Business, Christian Living, Love of God, Your Inheritance in Christ, Praying For Your Nation, and God's Grace.

The author has organised the Spirit of God through prayer topics to give you clarity and direction on how to pray for yourself and others effectively.

Whether you're just beginning your journey into prayer, or you are looking for a new way to gain a closer connection to God... This book will be a perfect assistant.

When praying the prayers in this book, make sure you pray fervently from your spirit. If you recite each one over and over again, expecting to get the same result, it will not be effective. You cannot plant a mango seed and expect to reap apple fruits. The Bible says, "Elias was a man subject to like passions as we are, and he prayed earnestly that it might not rain: and it rained not on the earth by the space of three years and six months" James 5:17.

Elijah had the very same result, as he prayed fervently with heartfelt passion. Each prayer in this book is designed to make you feel inspired by the Holy Spirit. As you pray, expect God to answer you and for there to be changes in the theme you want to target.

From God's Blessings to Happiness/Joy, this book is filled with incredibly helpful content.

Make sure you don't pray the prayers just once; you are free to say them as many times as possible. You want your prayer to be much like Elijah, as he prayed fervently and continuously. For example, you do not intercede for a sinner to get saved just once, you keep interceding until they give their life to Christ and are established in a local assembly. God is just waiting for you to pray these prayers with great faith in your heart. The Lord Jesus Christ said, "Therefore I tell you, what you ask for in prayer, believe that you have received it, and it will be yours" Mark 11:24.

So, what are you waiting for? Begin your new spiritual journey now!

DEDICATION

This book is dedicated to those looking to benefit from the power of prayer

Not sure where to start? Then this is the perfect book for you.

ABOUT THE AUTHOR

'The best way to predict the future is to create it...'

Selva Sugunendran is a writer and dedicated researcher and publisher on Alzheimer's. He was educated in London and has lived in the city for the past 50 years. He gained a degree in Electronic Engineering at Kingston University and has a Masters in NLP. He is also a Clinical Hypnotherapist and has two University diplomas in Alzheimer's and Prevention of Dementia.

Selva's working life included owning a high security software development company, but it has been his work with those who have succumbed to Dementia and Alzheimer's where he has made the greatest impact.

Since selling his business, Selva has written 23 books, including six bestsellers, with the latest ones being on the subject of Alzheimer's: Prevention of Dementia; Say No To Alzheimer's; Prevent, Delay, Reverse Alzheimer's; What You Need to Know About Dementia; You Can Beat Alzheimer's – Let Me Show You How; The Nature And Kinds Of Autism Including Asperger's Syndrome; followed recently by Empowering Healing & Hope Through Faith and Modern Day Healing Miracles to provide hope for those declared terminally ill. The current book titled "Prayer Is Powerful" is the latest book. They are all available on Amazon, along with Selva's other titles: https://geni.us/betterhealth

When he has time to himself, Selva enjoys cruising, flying, gliding and racing. He is also a great cricket fan and a car enthusiast, but a lot of his time is devoted to helping those who have fallen victim to the horrors of Alzheimer's and Dementia. He is a Dementia Champion for Alzheimers.org.uk.

In the future, Selva intends to continue with his work, fighting against Alzheimer's, writing books based on scientific, medical research and spiritual beliefs as well as continuing to lecture on the subject to as many people as he can.

ACKNOWLEDGEMENT

Last year, I felt truly blessed as I was able to publish two Christian books. The first book titled "Empowering Healing & Hope Through Faith" became a #1 Bestseller three times while my second book titled, "Modern Day Healing Miracles" became a Bestseller, too. I am so grateful to all those who bought these two books and the great feedback I received from them, including their nudging me to write a book on powerful prayers in daily life. So here it is—A book on 250 categorised powerful prayers.

Unfortunately, there is not enough room here to acknowledge each and every one of them. My special heartful thanks go to all those kind people.

Thanks also to my wife Kamini, my son Shaun, daughter(in-law) Florence Nishanthi and my two grandchildren Jason & Lisa, for their support, encouragement and understanding.

My heartful thanks also go to those that I couldn't mention. You know who you are!

I cannot end this acknowledgment without giving thanks to God, who has provided me with everything I need, as illustrated in Philippines 4: Verses 11-13

Author's Note:

I Pray for Your Faith, Your Boldness in Asking God As Well As Your determined Expectation For Fulfilment of His Promises.

Before You Delve Into the Book of 250 Prayers, Here Are a Few Very Important Bible Promises to Whet Your Appetite. Please Read Them At Least Once Before Moving on. God Bless.

"Do not be anxious about anything, but in everything by prayer and supplication with thanksgiving let your requests be made known to God. And the peace of God, which surpasses all understanding, will guard your hearts and your minds in Christ Jesus." **Philippians 4:6-7**

"And whatever you ask in prayer, you will receive, if you have faith." **Matthew 21:22**

"Ask, and it will be given to you seek, and you will find; knock, and it will be opened to you." **Matthew 7:7**

"Therefore, I tell you, whatever you ask in prayer, believe that you have received it, and it will be yours." **Mark 11:24**

And he said to them, "This kind cannot be driven out by anything but prayer." **Mark 9:29**

"Whatever you ask in my name, this I will do, that the Father may be glorified in the Son. If you ask me anything in my name, I will do it." **John 14:13-14**

"Praying at all times in the Spirit, with all prayer and supplication. To that end, keep alert with all perseverance, making supplication for all the saints." **Ephesians 6:18**

"But Peter put them all outside and knelt down and prayed; and turning to the body, he said, "Tabitha, arise." And she opened her eyes, and when she saw Peter, she sat up." **Acts 9:40**

"Is anyone among you sick? Let him call for the elders of the church, and let them pray over him, anointing him with oil in the name of the Lord.

And the prayer of faith will save the one who is sick, and the Lord will raise him up. And if he has committed sins, he will be forgiven. Therefore, confess your sins to one another and pray for one another, that you may be healed. The prayer of a righteous person has great power as it is working." **James 5:14-16**

THE BOOK OF 250 PRAYERS

Chapter 1: PRAYER OF THANKSGIVING

It is important you thank God for the wonderful things He has done for you. To be grateful or thankful is to ask God to do more for you. The Psalmist says for you to count your blessings, name them one by one, and it will surprise you what the Lord has done for you. When you can remember to thank God for what He did for you, there is nothing you would ask Him that He will not do for you.

In this category of prayers, the Spirit of God is going to guide you by showing you what it means to appreciate God. He will also show you so many things He has done for you. There are those who do not know exactly what to thank God for or how to thank Him. As you say the prayers in this category, the Holy Spirit will not only help you say thank You to God, but He will also open the eyes of your understanding to comprehend what you are doing. To thank God is more than just words, the thanksgiving must come out from your spirit; it must be heartfelt. If you are appreciative of little things, you will open the way for God to do bigger things for you. That is how important thanksgiving is to God. This is an opportunity for the Spirit of God to help you imbibe the attitude of thanksgiving to God. As you open your heart to Him, testimonies will abound in your life.

1. PRAYER OF THANKING GOD

Bible Passage

"*I will give thanks to the Lord because of his righteousness; I will sing the praises of the name of the Lord Most High*" Psalm 7: 17.

Father, my heart is filled with gratitude to You for all that You have done for me. I am grateful for Your protection, provisions, guidance and abilities You have granted me. Lord, I thank You for seeing my family and friends through the trying times with Covid-19. I thank You for not allowing the plague to come near our dwellings as You promised in Your Word. Lord, I appreciate Your grace, in Jesus' Name. Amen.

Further Reading: Psalm 9: 1.

2. THANK GOD FOR YOUR SALVATION

Bible Passage

"For it is by grace you have been saved, through faith--and this is not from yourselves, it is the gift of God not by works, so that no one can boast" Ephesians 2: 8 – 9.

Blessed Father, I thank You for my salvation; You plucked me out of the domain of darkness into the Kingdom of Your dear Son Jesus Christ. I thank You for loving me to be worthy of Your salvation. Now I am Your child, Your priced possession. I am now qualified to come into Your presence and bide there without any sense of guilt. I declare that I am born again; I am a child of God, in Jesus' Name. Amen.

Further Reading: 2 Timothy 1: 9.

3. THANK GOD FOR GIVING YOU ETERNAL LIFE

Bible Passage

"I give them eternal life, and they shall never perish; no one will snatch them out of my hand. My Father, who has given them to me, is greater than all; no one can snatch them out of my Father's hand. I and the Father are one" John 10: 28 – 30.

Precious Father, I am so grateful for granting me eternal life. Your Word says, "He that has the Son has life…" I have received the Lord Jesus Christ as my Lord and personal savior, I have Zoe, the very life of God beating behind my chest. Today, I declare that I enjoy all the benefits of the eternal life that I have. Sin or the devil does not have control over me. I am not susceptible to sickness, disease, infirmity or death because I have the life of God in me, in Jesus' Name. Amen.

Further Reading: 1 John 5: 11.

4. THANK GOD FOR GIVING ME THE HOLY SPIRIT

Bible Passage

"And I will ask the Father, and he will give you another advocate to help you and be with you forever... But the Advocate, the Holy Spirit, whom the Father will send in my name, will teach you all things and will remind you of everything I have said to you" John 14: 16; 26

I thank You so much Father, for giving me the Holy Spirit. The Holy Spirit is my Comforter, Intercessor, Advocate, Counselor, Helper, Strengthener, Teacher, Stand-by and Extraordinary Strategist. I can never be confused again because the Holy Spirit is always with me to help and counsel me. The Holy Spirit is the Father in me. Thus, I am never alone or without help. All that I need to know, the Holy Spirit will teach or bring to my remembrance, in Jesus' Name. Amen.

Further Reading: 1 Corinthians 3: 16.

5. THANK GOD FOR HIS WORD AND THE ABILITY TO UNDERSTAND IT

Bible Passage

"All Scripture is God-breathed and is useful for teaching, rebuking, correcting and training in righteousness, so that the servant of God may be thoroughly equipped for every good work" 2 Timothy 3: 16 – 17.

Lord God, the entrance of Your Word gives light and understanding to the simple. Thank You for giving me the ability to receive Your Word into my spirit and understand it anytime I study my Bible or hear Your Word preached. Lord Jesus, You said to Your disciples, 'To you, it is given the ability to understand the mystery of the Kingdom'. I thank You Father; I have that same ability today through the Holy Spirit. Glory to God! Amen.

Further Reading: Hebrews 4: 12.

6. THANK GOD FOR HIS ABUNDANCE GRACE IN YOUR LIFE

Bible Passage

"Who saved us and called us to a holy calling, not because of our works but because of his own purpose and grace, which he gave us in Christ Jesus before the ages began" 2 Timothy 1: 9.

Heavenly Father, thank You for the abundance of grace You have personally bestowed on me. You saved and called me into a holy calling in Christ, not by my human qualifications but by Your unique grace. Lord, by Your grace, I am doing exploits in ministry and in life generally. I receive favor and blessings because You have graced me with all that pertains to life and godliness. I am enjoying my life because of Your great grace in my life. Blessed be Your Holy Name Father, in Jesus' Name. Amen.

Further Reading: 2 Corinthians 8: 7.

7. THANK GOD FOR MY FAMILY, MARRIAGE AND CHILDREN

Bible Passage

"But if serving the LORD seems undesirable to you, then choose for yourselves this day whom you will serve, whether the gods your ancestors served beyond the Euphrates, or the gods of the Amorites, in whose land you are living. But as for me and my household, we will serve the LORD" Joshua 24: 15.

Lord God, I thank You in the Name of the Lord Jesus Christ for my family, marriage and children. I thank You because You surround us with Your wonderful love and glory. Your wall of protection surrounds us as the mountains surround Jerusalem. I thank You because my marriage is working; my children are healthy and doing great in their academics. Your peace garrisons my family to the glory of Your Holy Name. Blessed be Your Name Father. Amen.

Further Reading: Joshua 24: 16.

8. THANK GOD FOR HIS PEACE THAT YOU ENJOY IN YOUR LIFE

Bible Passage

"Now may the Lord of peace himself give you peace at all times in every way. The Lord be with you all" 2 Thessalonians 3: 16.

Lord, I thank You so much for Your peace that I enjoy in my life. You said in this world, we will have troubles, but we should take heart because You have overcome the world for us. You gave us peace that surpasses all human understanding. I declare that no matter the troubles and trials I face in this world, my heart is mantled with the peace of God. I refuse to fear or be shaken. I declare that I am always at peace, in Jesus' Name. Amen.

Further Reading: John 14: 27.

9. THANK GOD FOR BLESSING YOU WITH DIVINE HEALTH

Bible Passage

"He sent out his word and healed them, snatching them from the door of death" Psalm 107: 20.

Father, You said in Your Word that You desire that we prosper and live in health, even as my soul prospers. Glory to Your Name, Father! In the Name of the Lord Jesus Christ, I declare that the same Spirit that raised Jesus from the dead dwells in my mortal body; He vitalizes every fiber of my being. Every cell of my blood, bones, muscles and organs are made alive by the Holy Spirit that lives in me. Halleluiah!

Further Reading: 3 John 1: 2.

10. THANK GOD FOR YOUR JOB, BUSINESS AND FINANCES

Bible Passage

"You may say to yourself, "My power and the strength of my hands have produced this wealth for me." But remember the LORD your God, for it is he who gives you the ability to produce wealth, and so confirms his covenant, which he swore to your forefathers, as it is today" Deuteronomy 8: 17 -18.

Father God, I thank You for always having my best interest. You have blessed me with all that pertains to life and godliness. You gave me the strength to make wealth through my job, businesses and other avenues. Lord, I thank You because the Lord Jesus was poor so that through His poverty, I became rich. I declare that I am rich in Pounds, Dollars, Euro, in gold, silver and all the good things of life. I am blessed to be God's outreached-hand to bless others, in Jesus' Name. Amen.

Further Reading: Proverbs 10: 22.

11. THANK GOD FOR THE SAFETY AND SECURITY YOU ENJOY IN CHRIST

Bible Passage

"The Lord is my light and my salvation—whom shall I fear? The Lord is the stronghold of my life— of whom shall I be afraid?" Psalm 27: 1.

The Word of God says, 'except the Lord watches over a city, those who watch it do so in vain.' Safety is of the Lord. Thus, I thank You, Father, for my safety and security. In the world where there is so much trouble, insecurity and uncertainty, Lord, in You, I find safety in Jesus' Name. The Name of the Lord is a strong tower, the righteous run to it and is safe. My life is hidden in Christ, in God. I and all that are mine are secure in the mighty Name of the Lord Jesus Christ. Amen.

Further Reading: 2 Thessalonians 3: 3.

12. THANK GOD FOR THE BODY OF CHRIST IN YOUR LOCAL ASSEMBLY AND THE WORLD

Bible Passage

"Now I rejoice in my sufferings for your sake, and in my flesh I do my share on behalf of His body, which is the church, in filling up what is lacking in Christ's afflictions" **Colossians 1: 24.**

Precious Father, I thank You for the Body of Christ in my local church and all over the world. I thank You for granting us safety and guidance in these perilous times. I thank You for the peace and prosperity the church enjoys. I declare that Your church is marching on, and the gates of hell will never be able to prevail against it, in Jesus' Name. This is still the church age; therefore, I restrain the devil from running riot in our world till the church is raptured, in Jesus' Name. Amen.

Further Reading: 1 Corinthians 12: 27.

13. THANK GOD FOR GRANTING YOU HIS NATURE OF RIGHTEOUSNESS

Bible Passage

"God made him who had no sin to be sin for us, so that in him we might become the righteousness of God" 2 Corinthians 5: 21.

Dear Father, I thank You for granting me Your nature of righteousness. The Lord Jesus has made my righteousness, wisdom, sanctification and redemption. I declare that I am righteous, sanctified and holy. I refuse to entertain any thought of guilt or condemnation in my conscience. My heart is always filled with thoughts of righteousness, and I produce fruits of righteousness by the Spirit of God that lives in me. Righteousness is now my nature because I am born of God. Blessed be God. Halleluiah!

Further Reading: Proverbs 21: 21.

14. THANK GOD FOR THE PEACE AND PROSPERITY OF YOUR NATION

Bible Passage

"Also, seek the peace and prosperity of the city to which I have carried you into exile. Pray to the LORD for it, because if it prospers, you too will prosper" Jeremiah 29: 7.

Father, I thank You because due to Your mercies and love, my nation has been preserved from destruction. The plans of the enemy to cause pain, chaos and havoc with the so-called 'pandemic' were frustrated by Your Spirit. Lord, I thank You for honoring our prayers. I declare that our nation is coming out of these challenges stronger. Every section of our national lives is restored to full potential in the Name of the Lord Jesus Christ. Amen.

Further Reading: Psalm 122: 6.

15. THANK GOD FOR HIS LOVE THAT IS SHED ABROAD IN YOUR HEART

Bible Passage

"And hope does not disappoint us, because God has poured out His love into our hearts through the Holy Spirit, whom He has given us" Romans 5: 5.

Gracious Father, I am completely overwhelmed by Your liquid love that overflows in my heart. I declare that I can love anyone and everybody through the Spirit of God in me. I see people with the eyes of love, the same way God sees them. I love people regardless of the faults by the power of the Holy Spirit. My words, actions and opinions are coated with God's love. Through me, the love of God is manifested to others. I thank You, blessed Father in Jesus' Name. Amen.

Further Reading: 1 Corinthians 16: 14.

16. THANK GOD FOR THE PEOPLE IN YOUR LIFE; THOSE WHO INSPIRE AND ENCOURAGE YOU

Bible Passage

"Whoever walks with the wise becomes wise, but the companion of fools will suffer harm" Proverbs 13: 20.

Father, in the Name of the Lord Jesus Christ, I thank You for the people You have graciously placed in my life to be a blessing to me. These people have been a blessing, inspiration and encouragement to me in one way or another. You have used them to help me thus far in life, and I am so grateful. I pray that as they have been there for me, they will always find help and grace when they need them. They are blessed in all they do. The peace of God will always be with them, and they will experience Your power at work on their behalf. Amen.

Further Reading: Proverbs 27: 17.

17. THANK GOD FOR THE GIFT OF LIFE - FOR THE OPPORTUNITIES AND PRIVILLEGES HE HAS GIVEN YOU

Bible Passage

"We must work the works of Him who sent Me as long as it is day; night is coming when no one can work" John 9: 4.

Father, I thank You in the Name of the Lord Jesus Christ, for the gift of life, for the many opportunities and privileges You have granted me, both in ministry and in other facets of life. Father, in You I live, move and have my being. I declare that You are my source and sustainer. I thank You, Father, for using the opportunities and privileges to bless and enhance my life. I thank You, Most Holy Father. Halleluiah! Amen.

Further Reading: Ephesians 5: 16.

18. THANK GOD FOR THE SUCCESSES OF OTHERS

Bible Passage

"Do nothing out of selfish ambition or vain conceit. Rather, in humility value others above yourselves" Philippians 2: 3.

Precious Father, I sincerely express my thanks to You for the successes and achievements of folks in my world of contact. I thank You for their exploits in their endeavors. Lord, I thank You for those who have new babes, started new businesses and jobs, those who got promoted, those who got married, etc. Father God, I thank You for those whose lives You saved from the effects of the 'pandemic.' You are worthy to be praised. I thank You, Lord, in Jesus' Name. Amen.

Further Reading: Galatians 5: 26.

19. THANK GOD FOR THE POWER AND AUTHORITY YOU HAVE IN CHRIST JESUS

Bible Passage

"But you will receive power when the Holy Spirit comes on you; and you will be my witnesses in Jerusalem, and in all Judea and Samaria, and to the ends of the earth" Acts 1: 8.

Blessed Father, I am so thankful for the power and authority I have in Christ Jesus. You gave me the power to tread upon scorpions and serpents, power to heal the sick and raise the dead, power to cast devils and to wrought miracles. You made me a champion and a victor in this life. Father, I thank You for the authority to use the Name of Jesus to change situations and circumstances. With this power, I am the one in charge, the one cutting the shots by the power of the Holy Spirit, in Jesus' Name. Amen.

Further Reading: Matthew 10: 8.

20. THANK GOD FOR THE GIFT OF FAITH

Bible Passage

"For I say, through the grace given to me, to everyone who is among you, not to think of himself more highly than he ought to think, but to think soberly, <u>as God has dealt to each one a measure of faith</u>" Romans 12: 3.

Glory to God! The Word of God says faith is the victory that overcomes the world, even our faith. Father God, I thank You for giving me the gift of faith. I understand that faith is the currency in the kingdom of God. I thank You, Lord, because my faith is growing by the Word, and it is producing great results in my life. In the Name of the Lord Jesus, I make war with my faith; I fight the good fight of faith and always win. Halleluiah! Amen.

Further Reading: Romans 10: 17.

21. THE MIRACLES YOU EXPERINCE EVERY DAY

Bible Passage

"Jesus looked at them and said, "With man this is impossible, but with God all things are possible" Matthew 19: 26.

Heavenly Father, how grateful I am for the miracles I experience every day. I sleep every night and wake up strong and full of vitality. From the home to the office and the different hurdles I face daily, I come out better, a winner. Glory to Your Holy Name! I receive miracles in my finances, job and business effortlessly by the power of the Holy Spirit. Lord, I thank You for making me a wonder to my world. They have noticed that You are with me always and that it is by You I win in life. I thank You, Father, in Jesus' Name. Amen.

Further Reading: Matthew 17: 20.

Chapter 2: PRAYER FOR OVERCOMING TRIALS

A number of us have been taught to have a negative mindset towards trials. In other words, trials spell negativity, but that is not the attitude the Lord expects us to have about trials. He said to count it as all joy when we fall into trials. That means there is something joyful about the trials that come our way. The Scriptures let us know that God will not allow the trials we cannot bear to come to us. Put differently, the trials come to us because God expects us to use them to bring Him glory. Like someone rightly said, problems gravitate towards their solutions. Trials are life's examinations, and we must pass through them to move to the next level of life. As far as God is concerned, trials are our steps to climb to greater heights in life.

The prayers in this category help you to pray to overcome different kinds of trials. Trials are designed to come in different forms; some are from your mistakes, while others are as a result of persecution, fear, temptations, or rite of passage. Understand that God does not tempt anyone with evil, so trials cannot come from God. The Lord Jesus Christ asked us to pray so we will not fall into temptation. Likewise, the Word says if you fail on the day of a trial or adversity, your strength is small. So gear up and allow the Holy Spirit to help you pray to overcome every trial that will come to you in life because they are guaranteed to come to you.

22. PRAY AGAINST FEAR

Bible Passage

"*He will never leave you nor forsake you. Do not be afraid; do not be discouraged*" Deuteronomy 31: 8.

Dear Father, Your Word says that You have not given me the spirit of fear but the spirit of power, love and sound mind. I declare that I do not walk in fear. Every atom of fear in me is disabled in the Name of Jesus Christ. Therefore, I confront life with boldness, faith and clarity. I face every challenge, knowing that I am always a winner. I am more than a conqueror; I triumph perpetually in this life. I am conscious that no weapon that is fashioned against me shall ever prosper because God is with me strong. Halleluiah!

Further Reading: Isaiah 43: 1.

23. PRAY FOR WISDOM TO NAVIGATE THE TIMES WE ARE IN

Bible Passage

"Blessed is the man who remains steadfast under trial, for when he has stood the test he will receive the crown of life, which God has promised to those who love him" James 1: 12.

Blessed Father, I thank You for granting me divine wisdom to weather the storms raging in the times we are in. I declare that I am conscious of who I am. I am a child of God. The Lord Jesus Christ is my wisdom. I have the Word of God, which is the wisdom of God in my heart. I understand that these are perilous times, and I deal wisely. I am steadfast in trials because my focus is on the crown of life that is set for me in Jesus' Name. Amen.

Further Reading: Romans 8: 28.

24. PRAY NOT TO COMPROMISE

Bible Passage

Be strong in the Lord and in the power of His might. Put on the whole armor of God that you may be able to stand against the wiles of the devil. For we do not wrestle against flesh and blood, but against principalities, against powers, against rulers of the darkness of this age... Stand therefore, having girded your waist with truth, having on the breastplate of righteousness, and having shod your feet with the preparation of the gospel of peace; above all, taking the shield of faith with which you will be able to quench the fiery darts of the wicked one. Ephesians 6: 10-16

I ask for the strength and grace not to give in to social, emotional, financial, or mental pressure that might lead me to compromise your standards in my daily interactions with the world. Lord, receive your help not to say "Yes" when I should have said "No." I need the promised grace that offers salvation and can teach me to say "No" to ungodliness and worldly entanglements. There shall be a supply of divine strength and the ability to stand for what is right and pleasing to my God. I will not be intimidated to embrace or celebrate the unfruitful works of darkness in Jesus' name. I am empowered to live a self-controlled, upright, and godly life in this present age as I wait for the blessed hope. Amen.

Further Reading: 2 Timothy 2: 4, Matthew 6: 24

25. PRAYER FOR THE GRACE TO HANDLE ANY TRIAL

Bible Passage

"And after you have suffered a little while, the God of all grace, who has called you to his eternal glory in Christ, will himself restore, confirm, strengthen, and establish you" 1 Peter 5: 10.

I thank You, dear Father, for Your grace that is at work in me. Daily, I grow in grace, and I am able to handle any trial that I might face. I know that God will not allow the temptation or trial that I cannot bear to come to me. Every trial that I face is because I am the most qualified candidate for it. It came to me because I have its solution. I declare that every trial is bread for me; I will chew it up because it came to enhance me in Jesus' Name. Amen.

Further Reading: James 1: 2

26. PRAY TO BE ABLE TO SEE OPPORTUNITIES IN TRIALS

Bible Passage

"No temptation has taken you except what is common to man. God is faithful, who will not allow you to be tempted above what you are able, but will with the temptation also make the way of escape, that you may be able to endure it" 1 Corinthians 10: 13.

Every problem gravitates towards its solution. In the Name of the Lord Jesus Christ, I see opportunities that come with every trial or challenge. Rather than getting worked up or beaten down by any trial, I see the glory that follows it, just like the Lord Jesus who has to bear the Cross and its shame because of the glory that followed. I do not see the troubles or pains but the opportunities it brings. I thank You, Father God. Halleluiah!

Further Reading: 1 Peter 4: 12 – 13.

27. PRAY FOR CHRISTIANS FACING DIFFERENT FORMS OF TRIALS

Bible Passage

"I have said these things to you, that in me you may have peace. In the world you will have tribulation. But take heart; I have overcome the world" John 16: 33.

Father, I pray for Christians around the world that are facing difficult times or trials because they process Your Name. Lord God, I pray that their hearts be mantled with faith and understanding so that they do not lose their salvation. The Word of God that they have learnt would come alive in their spirits; they would war with the Word and remain strong in faith. I pray for help for them and divine deliverance by the power of the Holy Spirit in Jesus' Name. Amen.

Further Reading: Romans 12: 12.

28. PRAY FOR CHRISTIANS IN TROUBLED TERRITORIES IN THE WORLD: THAT THEIR FAITH DOES NOT FAIL THEM IN THEIR TRIALS

Bible Passage

"Even though I walk through the valley of the shadow of death, I will fear no evil, for you are with me; your rod and your staff, they comfort me" Psalm 23: 4.

Father God, You are the strong and breasted One. You are the God that can save and deliver Your people. I pray for my Christian brothers and sisters in troubled territories in the world. I pray for their safety and deliverance from the troubles that constantly surround them. I pray and declare that they are shielded from the arrows and darts of the enemy against them. No weapon formed against them shall prosper in Jesus' Name. Amen.

Further Reading: Romans 8: 18.

29. PRAY FOR COURAGE IN THE FACE OF PERSECUTION

Bible Passage

"Therefore do not throw away your confidence, which has a great reward" Hebrews 10:35

Father, I thank You for granting me the spirit of courage. In the face of severe persecutions, I am courageous to maintain my faith in Christ Jesus. The Lord Jesus said that we would be persecuted because of Him and that in this world, we would have troubles. The good news is that He has overcome the world and its systems for me. I know that God is with me always; thus my heart is filled with courage in Jesus' Name. Amen.

Further Reading: 1 Peter 1: 6.

30. MAKE DECLARATIONS – AFFIRMING YOUR VICTORY OVER THE ENEMY

Bible Passage

"But he said to me, "My grace is sufficient for you, for my power is made perfect in weakness." Therefore I will boast all the more gladly of my weaknesses, so that the power of Christ may rest upon me" 2 Corinthians 12: 9.

In the Name of the Lord Jesus Christ, I affirm that I am a victor in this life. I am an overcomer, more than a conqueror. I walk in perpetual victory over the enemy. I declare that though I walk through the valley of the shadow of death, I fear no evil. The rod and the staff of God comfort me. When the enemies compasses against me, they stumble and fall. When they come against me in one way, they flee in seven ways by the power of the Holy Spirit at work in me. Amen.

Further Reading: Philippians 4: 13.

31. PRAY FOR HOPE IN TRIALING TIMES

Bible Passage

"Therefore, my heart is glad, and my glory rejoices; my flesh also will rest in hope." Psalm 16: 9.

Dear Lord God, I thank You because my heart is glad and my glory rejoices; in the Name of the Lord Jesus Christ, I declare that my flesh rests in hope. My heart refuses to fret because of the plague, deceptions and confusion that have befallen the world. My hope is in You, Father, and in the Name of the Lord Jesus Christ; I declare that I am an overcomer in this life. I am a child of God; thus, I live above the system of this world. Halleluiah! Amen.

Further Reading: Psalm 119: 114.

32. PRAY FOR THE PEACE OF GOD

Bible Passage

"I have said these things to you, that in me you may have peace. In the world you will have tribulation. But take heart; I have overcome the world." John 16: 33.

I pray that the Lord of peace Himself gives me peace at all times in every way. That the Lord be with me at all times. I declare that His peace garrisons my heart so that the evil and pressures that affect the children of this world do not affect me. Lord, my mind stays on Your Word and its promises. Therefore, I know that I cannot be moved. Praise be unto Your holy Name Father. Amen.

Further Reading: 2 Thessalonians 3: 16.

33. PRAY THAT THE WORD OF GOD WILL DOMINATE YOUR HEART: IT WILL HELP YOU OVERCOME TRIALS

Bible Passage

"Let the word of Christ dwell in you richly in all wisdom, teaching and admonishing one another in psalms and hymns and spiritual songs, singing with grace in your hearts to the Lord" Colossians 3: 16.

Lord God, I thank You for Your Word that dwells richly in my heart. Like the Lord Jesus who had to use Your Word to checkmate the devil when He was tempted, likewise, I fill my heart with Your Word to use on the evil day. I will call forth the Word from my spirit to war. The Word of God is the Sword of the Spirit; it is my weapon to war when I face trials in Jesus' Name. Amen.

Further Reading: Romans 10: 17.

34. PRAY THAT THE RIGHTEOUS WILL HAVE THE OPPORTUNITIES IN GOVERNMENT

Bible Passage

"When the righteous are in authority, the people rejoice: but when the wicked bears rule, the people mourn" Proverbs 29: 2.

Lord God, I pray that the righteous would find more opportunities in governments of their countries. Your Word says when the righteous rule, the people rejoice. I declare that they would be bold to take steps into governance. All that they need; the men, materials, finance, logistics, information and connections are made available to them in Jesus' Name. I pray that all the sensitive positions are taken over by born-again Christians who would use their opportunities to enhance the furtherance of the Gospel through the power of the Holy Spirit. Blessed be God forevermore. Amen.

Further Reading: Proverbs 28: 15.

35. PRAY AGAINST PHYSICAL AND SPIRITUAL ATTACKS ON CHRISTIANS

Bible Passage

"No weapon that is formed against you shall prosper; and every tongue that shall rises against you in judgment you shall condemn. This is the heritage of the servants of the LORD, and their righteousness is of me, said the LORD" Isaiah 54: 17.

Father, in the Name of the Lord Jesus, I come against spiritual and physical attacks on Christians, especially in my country. I raise a standard against the attackers in Jesus' Name. I declare that my Christian brothers and sisters are protected, preserved, fortified in the Name of Jesus. I nullify every attack and declare they are turned to naught by the power of the Holy Spirit. Just as the mountains are round about Jerusalem, so the Lord is His people to protect them. Amen.

Further Reading: Isaiah 45: 24.

36. PRAY AGAINST OBNOXIOUS LAWS AND POLICIES THAT ARE MEANT TO SET CHRISTIANS UP FOR PERSECUTION

Bible Passage

"Submit yourselves for the Lord's sake to every human institution, whether to the king as the supreme authority, or to governors, who are sent by him to punish those who do wrong and to commend those who do right" 1 Peter 2: 13 – 14.

Father, I pray in the Name of the Lord Jesus against laws and government policies that are made in different clans to set Your children up for persecutions. I declare that all such laws and policies are repelled; I declare them null and void by the power of the Holy Spirit. I pray that men and women are rising up to challenge these laws and policies, and they are highly favored in their course. Speedily, every such ordinance is repelled. Glory to God!

Further Reading: Romans 13: 3 – 4.

37. PRAY AGAINST THE PLANS OF UNREASONABLE AND WICKED PEOPLE AGAINST THE BODY OF CHRIST

Bible Passage

"And that we may be delivered from unreasonable and wicked men; for not all have faith" 2 Thessalonians 3: 2.

Father God, by the power of the Holy Spirit at work in me, I spoil every work or plan of unreasonable and wicked men against the Body of Christ. No matter how highly placed, sophisticated and powerful the people are, I shatter them in Jesus' Name. Amen. I curse their sources; I pronounce them dead. I cut off their influence, and I command their hearts to fail them. They lose every atom of courage in them in Jesus' Name. Amen.

Further Reading: Romans 15: 31.

38. PRAY FOR DIVINE DELIVERANCE FOR CHRISTIANS WRONGLY HELD AGAINST THEIR WILL FOR THE SAKE OF THE GOSPEL

Bible Passage

"So Peter was kept in prison, but the church was earnestly praying to God for him" Acts 12: 5.

Precious Father, I pray for Your divine deliverance for Christians wrongly held against their will and persecuted because of their faith in Christ. I pray that help and deliverance come to them. I dispatch ministry angels to orchestrate their release and freedom. In the Name of the Lord Jesus Christ, I command confusion in the camp of their captures; I withhold their peace until they release every member of the Body of Christ in their custody. Amen.

Further Reading: Matthew 18: 19.

39. PRAY FOR CHRISTIANS IN HOSTILE COMMUNITIES OR COUNTRIES: THAT THEY WOULD BE PROTECTED AGAINST ANY HARM

Bible Passage

"Keep me as the apple of your eye; hide me in the shadow of your wings from the wicked who are out to destroy me, from my mortal enemies who surround me" Psalm 17: 8 – 9.

Father, I thank You for Christians who live or work in hostile communities, countries or places where the devil has stirred the folks against Christians. I declare that they are constantly protected and that no harm will ever come to them. I pray that they find unique favor in the sight of the governments, security agents and people of great influence and importance in those clans to speak in their favor. I pray that Your mighty Hand of protection be upon them in Jesus' Name. Amen.

Further Reading: Deuteronomy 31: 6.

40. PRAY FOR MINISTERS OF THE GOSPEL BEING PERSECUTED FOR THE SAKE OF CHRIST

Bible Passage

"Now I exhort you, brothers, by our Lord Jesus Christ and by the love of the Spirit, to strive together with me in the prayers for me to God" Romans 15: 30.

Lord God, I thank You for the lives and families of the ministers of the Gospel. I pray for those facing great persecutions right now because they work in Your vineyard. I pray that they are vindicated from all the false accusations against them. I declare that those persecuting them be confounded and brought to shame in Jesus' Name. Lord, I pray that more doors of opportunities be opened for them and increase wisdom and courage for them so that they would speak Your Word boldly with the power of the Holy Spirit in Jesus' Name. Amen.

Further Reading: 2 Corinthians 12: 10.

41. PRAY FOR FOCUS AND NOT TO BE DISTRACTED FROM THE RACE THAT IS SET BEFORE YOU

Bible Passage

"Therefore we also, since we are surrounded by so great a cloud of witnesses, let us lay aside every weight, and the sin which so easily ensnares us, and let us run with endurance the race that is set before us" Hebrews 12: 1.

Father, I thank You for helping me to keep focused on the race that is set before me. I declare that nothing shall be able to separate me from the love of Christ. I am set on the course I must follow in the Name of the Lord Jesus Christ. I refuse to be distracted by the devil, sin, illness, men, economy or any circumstances. The Holy Spirit guards my steps in the right direction I should walk in Jesus' Name. Amen.

Further Reading: 1 Corinthians 9: 26.

42. PRAY THAT YOUR STRENGTH WILL NOT FAIL YOU IN THE DAY OF ADVERSITY

Bible passage

"If you faint in the day of adversity, your strength is small" Proverbs 24: 10.

Father God, blessed is Your Holy Name! I thank You for sending the Holy Spirit to be my strengthener. I declare that I am constantly strengthened by my Strengthener, the Holy Spirit. My faith is getting stronger as I study and meditate on the Word of God daily. No adversity is strong enough to shake me because my feet are deeply rooted on the Word of God. I thank You, Holy Father, in Jesus' Name. Amen.

Further Reading: Hebrews 12: 3.

43. PRAY AGAINST THE ATTACKS OF THE ENEMY

Bible Passage

"Through You, we will push back our adversaries, through Your name we will trample down those who rise up against us" Psalm 44: 5.

Father, through the authority and power in the Name of Jesus Christ, I declare that we will push back the enemy of the church and all Christians. Yes, in Your Name, we will trample down those who rise up against us. We cut them off from their roots and declare that they are forever dismantled. We seize their courage and render their power and influence useless. Even as they gather against us because their gathering is not of You, they scatter in pieces in Jesus' Name. Amen.

Further Reading: Psalm 34: 17.

44. PRAY TO BE ABLE TO RESIST THE DEVIL AT ALL TIMES

Bible Passage

"Submit yourselves, then, to God. Resist the devil, and he will flee from you" James 4: 7.

Lord God, Your Word says if I resist the devil, he will flee from me. You put in the devil what will make him flee at my resistance. From the temptation of Jesus, I learnt that with Your Word in my spirit and mouth, the devil cannot withstand me. Your Word in my mouth is the sword of the Spirit to put the devil to flight. As I speak forth Your Word, the devil and his cohorts are confounded; they are set in disarray in Jesus' Name. Amen.

Further Reading: Ephesians 4: 27.

45. PRAY THAT THE HOLY SPIRIT WILL BE WITH YOU THROUGH TRIALS

Bible Passage

"When they call on me, I will answer; I will be with them in trouble. I will rescue and honor them" Psalm 91: 15.

Father, You said in Your Word that You would never leave or forsake me. I thank You for sending the Holy Spirit to be with me till the end. I pray that in trials, I will recognize that You are with me in the Holy Spirit. I declare that I will not be distracted or overwhelmed to the point I will forget that You are always with me. I will call on You, Lord, and You will answer and save me from trouble in Jesus' Name. Amen.

Further Reading: Psalm 50: 15.

46. PRAY THAT NO TRIAL WILL OVERWHELM YOU OR DEFEAT YOU

Bible Passage

"No temptation has overtaken you that is not common to man. ... But God is faithful; he will not allow you to be tempted beyond what you are able, but with the temptation he will also provide a way out so that you may be able to bear it" 1 Corinthians 10: 13.

Lord, I thank You because You will never allow the trials that I cannot bear to come to me. You have made a victor and more than a conqueror. I triumph over every trial by the power of the Holy Spirit. No trial will be able to overwhelm or defeat me because greater is He that is in me than he that is in the world. The Lord Jesus has already overcome the world on my behalf. I have been declared the winner to the glory and praise of God. I thank You, Father, in Jesus' Name. Amen.

Further Reading: Matthew 6: 13.

47. PRAY FOR THE BODY OF CHRIST AT THESE CRITICAL TIMES

Bible Passage

"Praying at all times in the Spirit, with all prayer and supplication. To that end keep alert with all perseverance, making supplication for all the saints" Ephesians 6: 18.

Father God, in the Name of the Lord Jesus Christ, I pray for the Body of Christ all over the world. I declare that they are alert and watchful. I pray that their hearts are guided by the Word of God so that they are not swayed or deceived by the deceptions going on in the world presently. I declare that their hearts are garrisoned with the peace of God; they are strong in the Lord by the power of the Holy Spirit. Amen.

Further Reading: Acts 2: 42.

48. PRAY AGAINST THE WICKED SCHEMES OF THE ENEMY

Bible Passage

"Though they intended evil against you and devised a plot, they will not succeed" Psalm 21: 11.

Father, I pray against the wicked schemes of the enemy against me and all that has to do with me. Lord, Your Word says if they come against me in one way, they will flee in seven ways. You would give Your angels charge over me so that I will never dash my foot against a stone. By Your Spirit, I am circumspect, so I do not make mistakes the devil can capitalize on to my disadvantage in Jesus' Name. Amen.

Further Reading: Micah 2: 1.

49. PRAY FOR FREEDOM

Bible passage:

Stand fast therefore in the liberty by which Christ has made us free, and do not be entangled again with a yoke of bondage. Galatians 5: 1

I thank you because I am no longer a slave of fears, sicknesses, sins, or Satan. I am free to live a life of purpose. No chains can hold me back; I cannot be imprisoned in the nest of doubts and anxieties; I am more than a conqueror because the fullness of God dwells in me. I declare that my yokes are broken, barriers of progress are shattered, and the mountains standing in the path of my destiny are moved. Everything will work together for my good in Jesus' name, amen.

Further Reading: John 8: 36, Psalm 119: 45,

Chapter 3: PRAYERS TO OVERCOME WRONG HABITS

There is no bad habit you cannot do away with if you are really determined to stop it. No matter how deep it is eating into you or you are addicted to it, you can overcome it if you really want to. The Word of God says there is nothing impossible to him that believes. In other words, you can walk out of that habit before it destroys you. No matter how highly you are anointed, if you have a bad habit you are struggling with, before long, it will bring you down if you do not prayerfully handle it now. The Bible talked about the little foxes that spoil the vine. This can be likened to habits that inhibit prayers, the anointing, grace, faith, or bring disgrace and shame. Stop that struggle today. With faith, say these prayers, and you will be free to serve God.

The very first step to overcoming the wrong habits is through prayer. Through the prayers in this category, the Holy Spirit will guide you to pray to overcome whatever wrong habits you must remove from your life. The Word of God says that the effectual heartfelt, fervent prayer of the righteous avails. This is what saying the prayers in this group will do for you. Every wrong habit will fizzle out of your life unnoticed by the Spirit of God at work in you. That anger, bitterness, jealousy, greed, pornography, prayerlessness, forsaking the assembly of the brethren, etc., will leave effortlessly.

50. DECLARE THAT YOU CANNOT BE ADDICTED TO ANYTHING

Bible Passage

"For everything in the world—the lust of the flesh, the lust of the eyes, and the pride of life—comes not from the Father but from the world" 1 John 2: 16.

In the matchless Name of the Lord Jesus Christ and by the power of the Holy Spirit at work in me, I declare I cannot be addicted to anything. I have an inherent power of the Holy Spirit at work in me to stop any habit that I do not like or that is detrimental to my salvation. The only things I am addicted to are things that produce the fruits of righteousness, things that bring glory to God and edify my spirit, soul and body. Glory to God!

Further Reading: James 4: 7.

51. DECLARE THAT YOU HAVE OVERCOME EVERY WRONG HABIT IN YOUR LIFE

Bible Passage

"I have the right to do anything," you say—but not everything is beneficial. "I have the right to do anything"—but I will not be mastered by anything" 1 Corinthians 6: 12.

I declare in the Name of the Lord Jesus Christ, I am an overcomer in this world. I have overcome every wrong habit that hitherto ruled my life. I have overcome the spirit's anger, lies, greed, fornication, backbiting, drunkenness, etc. I refuse to be held down by any habit that would make me commit sin against God. The life of God that I have in me makes me a wonder, an overcomer in this life. Blessed be God!

Further Reading: 1 Corinthians 10: 13 – 14.

52. ASK GOD TO FORGIVE YOU OF THE SINS YOU COMMITTED DUE TO WRONG HABITS

Bible Passage

"Whoever conceals their sins does not prosper, but the one who confesses and renounces them finds mercy" Proverbs 28: 13.

Everlasting Father, I obtain forgiveness for all the willful sins I committed as a result of the wrong habits I was involved in. I refuse to be tied to any of the habits again. I live my life pleasing You. The life that I live now is not a life dented with sins but a life of righteousness. Sin does not have dominion over me anymore. I refuse to feel condemned or guilty because the Lord Jesus Christ has purged me of all unrighteousness. I thank You, Lord, in Jesus' Name. Amen.

Further Reading: Psalm 32: 5.

53. PRAY FOR THE COURAGE TO FORGIVE YOURSELF

Bible Passage

"*Casting all your anxieties on him, because he cares for you*" 1 Peter 5: 7.

I thank You, dear Father, for granting me courage to live free of guilt. I forgive myself for the wrongs I did in the past. Father, Your Word says even if my conscience condemns me, You are greater than my conscience, and You know all things. I thank You, Lord, for forgiving all my wrongs, and I take cue from that to forgive myself. I declare that I am free and in charge of my emotions in Jesus' Name. Amen.

Further Reading: 1 John 1: 9.

54. ASK FOR GOD'S GRACE TO BE ABLE TO RECOGNIZE THE WRONG HABITS TO REPENT OF

Bible Passage:

"It teaches us to say "No" to ungodliness and worldly passions and to live self-controlled, upright and godly lives in this present age" Titus 2: 12.

Gracious Father, I pray that going forward, I am able to recognize wrong habits no matter how subtle they are. I declare that I am equipped with the Word not to indulge in them. I repent of any wrong habit that I may unknowingly still indulge in. I recognize them by the Holy Spirit to repent of, in Jesus' Name. The grace of God is at work mightily in my life, and by it, every wrong habit is exposed to me by the power of the Holy Spirit and in the Name of Jesus Christ. Amen.

Further Reading: Colossians 3: 8.

55. PRAY AND REPENT WRONG SPIRITUAL HABITS. E.G. LAZY TO PRAY; SKIPPING CHURCH SERVICES, ETC.

Bible Passage

"Let us not neglect meeting together, as some have made a habit, but let us encourage one another, and all the more as you see the Day approaching" Hebrews 10: 25.

The Lord Jesus Christ commands us to pray always. The Apostle Paul also reiterates the need for us to pray without ceasing. The Word of God likewise warned us that we should not neglect meeting together, as some have made a habit, but let us encourage one another, and all the more as you see the Day approaching. Lord God, I pray for forgiveness, and I repent of these wrong habits and any other I might not be aware of in the Name of the Lord Jesus Christ. Amen.

Further Reading: Acts 2: 42.

56. ASK GOD FOR THE ABILITY TO REPLACE EVERY WRONG HABIT WITH GODLY HABITS

Bible Passage

"Do not lie to each other, <u>since you have taken off your old self with its practices</u>" 1 John 3: 9.

Lord God, I recognize by Your Spirit that the best way to heal from wrong habits is to replace them with godly ones. I ask for that ability today. In the Name of the Lord Jesus Christ, I have taken off my old self with its practices. I am dead to sin and alive unto God. I now live the life of righteousness. Praise God, old things are passed away, and all things have become new by the Spirit God. Blessed be God!

Further Reading: Colossians 3: 9 – 10.

57. PRAY AGAINST THE NEGATIVE CONSEQUENCES OF THE WRONG HABITS YOU WERE INVOLED IN

Bible Passage

"For he who does wrong will receive the consequences of the wrong which he has done, and that without partiality" Colossians 3: 25.

Father, in the Name of the Lord Jesus Christ, I pray that I will not be caught up with the negative consequences of the wrong habits I was hitherto involved in. Father, Your Word says that 'if any man be in Christ, he is a new creation, old things are passed away, behold all things have become new.' I declare that I will not suffer any negative consequences in my health, relationships, marriage, job, spiritual life, etc. It is not by power or might but by the Spirit of God in me. Halleluiah!

Further Reading: Galatians 6: 5.

58. DECLARE THAT YOU ARE FERVENT IN SPIRIT SERVING THE LORD

Bible Passage

"Not slothful in business; fervent in spirit; serving the Lord" Romans 12: 11.

Glory to God! In the Name of the Lord Jesus Christ, I declare that I am fervent in spirit, serving the Lord. I refuse to be cold or lukewarm least I get left out by the Lord. I am hot for the Gospel; I am a fanatic in advancing the Kingdom of God here on earth. In the Name of Jesus Christ, my passion, skills, finances, energy, etc., are for the promotion of Jesus Christ and His redemptive work for mankind. I am an ardent soul winner. Praise God!

Further Reading: Matthew 24: 12.

59. DECLARE THAT NO SIN OR HABIT EASILY BESET YOU ANYMORE

Bible Passage

"Therefore, since we are surrounded by such a great cloud of witnesses, let us throw off everything that hinders and the sin that so easily entangles. And let us run with perseverance the race marked out for us" Hebrews 12: 1.

In the Name of the Lord Jesus Christ, I declare that I am the righteousness of God in Christ Jesus. I am holy, sanctified and righteous. I am dead to sin and alive unto righteousness. My thoughts are righteous thoughts continually. I recognize who I am in Jesus Christ. Thus, I declare by the power of the Holy Spirit at work in me that the prince of this world comes, but he has nothing in me. No sin has any hold on me or can easily beset me. Praise God forevermore.

Further Reading: Romans 13: 12.

60. PRAY THAT THE WORD OF GOD WILL HENCEFORTH DOMINATE YOUR MIND

Bible Passage

"Therefore everyone who hears these words of mine and puts them into practice is like a wise man who built his house on the rock" Matthew 7: 24.

Glory to God, my Father! Lord God, I pray that Your Word dwells in me richly in all wisdom and spiritual understanding. My heart is filled with Your Word so that it is only Your Word I am yielded to. As I study or listen to Your Word and do them, I declare that it will enter my spirit and dominate my mind. It will be my mind influencer on any issue. Lord, Your Word is the light that illuminates my paths, including the thoughts of my heart. I thank You, Lord, in Jesus' Name. Amen.

Further Reading: Psalm 119: 9.

61. PRAY THAT NO HABIT CAN SEPARATE FROM THE LOVE OF GOD

Bible Passage

"Who shall separate us from the love of Christ? Shall trouble or hardship or persecution or famine or nakedness or danger or sword?" Romans 8: 35.

Heavenly Father, I pray that nothing shall be able to separate me from Your love, not even a habit, no matter how exciting it is. I declare that I am a child of God; I am in an inseparable union with the Father, Son and the Holy Spirit. In the Name of the Lord Jesus, I resist anything that would want to separate me from this oneness with the Godhead. Father, I am grateful I am accepted in the beloved. Father, glory to your Holy Name forevermore! Halleluiah!

Further Reading: Romans 8: 37

62. ASK FOR THE WISDOM TO AVOID THE WRONG COMPANY THAT CAN LURE YOU BACK TO WRONG HABITS

Bible Passage

"Do not be misled: "Bad company corrupts good character" 1 Corinthians 15: 33.

Lord God, I thank You for the friends and acquaintances I have in my sphere of contact. I pray for the wisdom to know the right ones to associate with and the wrong ones to avoid. I declare that I am the one influencing my friends, colleagues and acquaintances with the Gospel of Jesus Christ and not them luring me into sin. By the power of the Holy Spirit at work in me, I attract them to the good life, the life of God that I live in Jesus' Name. Amen.

Further Reading: Proverbs 22: 25.

63. PRAY FOR YOUNG PEOPLE THAT ARE BEING DESTROYED BY DRUG ADDICTION

Bible Passage

"*Do not be deceived: "Evil company corrupts good habits"* 1 Corinthians 15: 33.

Precious Father, Your Word said in Luke 17: 2, "It would be better for them to be thrown into the sea with a millstone tied around their neck than to cause one of these little ones to stumble."

Lord, I pray for children that the wicked folks have lured with drugs, and now they are addicted. They are now abusing drugs, sex, alcohol and other substances like second nature. Lord, I pray for their rescue and deliverance by the power of the Holy Spirit in Jesus' Name. Amen.

Further Reading: Proverbs 22: 25.

64. PRAY FOR GOD'S MINISTERS THAT ARE BEING DRAGGED TO SHAME AND DESTRUCTION BY WRONG HABITS

Bible Passage

"Lo, God will not reject a man of integrity, nor will He support the evildoers" Job 8: 20.

Father, I thank You for the men and women You have called into ministry. I pray that they remain as shining examples to their flocks. I pray that they realize the consequences of the wrong habits they are engaged in. And as many as detest these bad habits, they receive the ability to walk out of them in Jesus' Name. Lord, I pray that they will not cause You to reject them because You do not support evildoers. Amen.

Further Reading: Psalm 26: 5.

65. PRAY FOR GOD'S CHILDREN WHO ARE SECRETLY INDULGING IN WRONG HABITS

Bible Passage

"Make sure that none of you suffers as a murderer, or thief, or evildoer, or a troublesome meddler" 1 Peter 4: 15.

Father God, I pray for Your children all over the world who are secretly indulging in wrong habits that they realize that what they are doing in secret will bring them public disgrace. I pray for grace for each and every one of them to desist from these wrongs and turn their focus and passion to You. I declare that nothing shall separate them from Your love. I thank You Father in Jesus' Name. Amen.

Further Reading: Psalm 34: 16.

66. PRAY FOR THOSE IN YOUR WORLD OF CONTACT WHO ARE ADDICTED TO THE WRONG STUFF

Bible Passage

"Or do you not know that the unrighteous will not inherit the kingdom of God? Do not be deceived: neither the sexually immoral, nor idolaters, nor adulterers, nor men who practice homosexuality" 1 Corinthians 6: 9.

Lord God, I pray for my friends, acquaintances and those in my world of contact who are addicted to drugs, porn, alcohol, prostitution, rumor mugging, lying, bitterness, etc. I pray that the light of the glorious Gospel of Christ shines on them, that they receive Christ into their hearts and be saved. They will convert the passion and energy they have for these wrong habits to serving the Lord Jesus and moving His Kingdom forward. Praise God!

Further Reading: 1 Peter 2: 12.

67. ASK FOR GOD'S HELP FOR CHILDREN WHO WERE LURED INTO PROSTITUTION AND DRUGS AROUND THE WORLD

Bible Passage

"It would be better for them to be thrown into the sea with a millstone tied around their neck than to cause one of these little ones to stumble" Luke 17: 2.

Father God, I thank You for little children who some unscrupulous individuals are causing to do terrible things. They are made to get involved in things like prostitution, drug abuse, pornography, terrorism, armed robbery, stealing, gambling, etc. I pray for Your mighty Hand of deliverance to rescue these children. I pray that government agencies responsible for their protection will swing into action for their sake. I declare that the folks responsible for their slavery are brought to book in Jesus' Name. Amen.

Further Reading: Isaiah 40: 11.

68. PRAY FOR THE REHABS IN YOUR COMMUNITY THAT THEY ARE GRANTED GOD'S WISDOM TO HELP THEIR PATIENTS

Bible Passage

"But I will restore your health and heal your wounds, declares the LORD, because they call you an outcast, Zion, for whom no one cares" Jeremiah 30: 17.

Gracious Father, I pray for the rehabilitation centers where a lot of the folks recovering from addictions are being treated and helped. I pray for Your guidance and wisdom for those operating or working at these centers. I declare that they know what to do with each patient so that they can get maximum recovery. I pray for a quick recovery for the patients. And as they recover, the Spirit of God will guide them to replace the wrong addictions and habits with godly activities in Jesus' Name. Amen.

Further Reading: Jeremiah 8: 22.

69. THANK GOD FOR THE FREEDOM YOU HAVE TO SERVE HIM WITHOUT THE INHIBITIONS OF WRONG HABITS

Bible Passage

"This issue arose because some false brothers had come in under false pretenses to spy on our freedom in Christ Jesus, in order to enslave us" Galatians 2: 4.

Precious Father, I thank You for the freedom I have to serve You without any inhibitions or restrictions. I declare that those spying at my freedom are confounded. All their plans to frustrate me are brought to naught by the power of the Holy Spirit. I serve God with a clean heart and conscience without any feeling of guilt or condemnation. I declare that I am the conveyor of God's divine presence everywhere I go in Jesus' Name. Amen.

Further Reading: 1 John 2: 24.

Chapter 4: PRAYERS TO GROWING IN THE WORD

All you will ever need to succeed in life as a Christian or child of God are all wrapped up in the Word of God. The Word brings illumination, direction, enlightenment, understanding, freedom, and so much more. A good understanding of the Word of God will set you at liberty, free from the bondage of ignorance and errors. Remember what the Lord Jesus Christ said, 'You err because you do not know the scriptures.' When you study and meditate on the Word, your error will be minimal.

The Word of God cleanses like pure water. It sanctifies and delivers you into your inheritance. It can build you up into an edifice and give you the mindset of the just. With the Word in your heart, your thoughts would be sanctified and your words seasoned with grace. It is the Word of God that brings you hopes for the future and faith for the now. It is the Word, you can never fail in life. It will bring you success and great prosperity.

In this category, you will pray to grow in God's Word as well as the advancement of the Word around the world. From some of the importance of the Word above, you can see that it is important to pray to grow in the Word. Your prayer will inspire an appetite that will enable you to study and meditate on the Word always. Your prayer will also cause the Word to grow and spread around the world.

70. PRAY FOR THE MINISTERS OF THE GOSPEL

Bible Passage

"Pray also for me that whenever I speak, words may be given me so that I will fearlessly make known the mystery of the gospel" Ephesians 6: 19.

Dear Father, I pray for the ministers of the Gospel all over the world that their hearts are filled with wisdom, boldness and faith. I pray that whenever they open their mouths to speak Your Word, they would be fearless to learn the mystery of the Gospel. I declare that great and effective doors in ministry will continually be opened to them. I pray that they will always stand for and speak the truth with power in Jesus' Name. Amen.

Further Reading: 1 Thessalonians 5: 25.

71. PRAY FOR MORE LABORERS

Bible Passage

"And He was saying to them, "The harvest is plentiful, but the laborers are few; therefore beseech the Lord of the harvest to send out laborers into His harvest" Luke 10: 2.

Gracious Father, I pray for more laborers for the harvest of souls. I declare that in drones, men and women are pouring into the kingdom of God; they are giving their lives to the Lord Jesus being convicted by the Holy Spirit. I pray that souls all over the world would recognize the times we are in, the time of salvation, and by the Spirit receives salvation. More Christians are waking up to their soul winning responsibilities in Jesus' Name. Amen.

Further Reading: Matthew 20: 1.

72. PRAY THAT YOU WOULD GAIN MASTERY OF THE WORD

Bible Passage

"Likewise, a competitor does not receive the crown unless he competes according to the rules" 2 Timothy 2: 5.

Father, in the Name of the Lord Jesus Christ, I declare that as I study and put Your Word to practice on a daily basis, I will gain mastery of it. Your Word says I should not be a hearer only but a doer of Your Word. I make Your Word foolproof in every area of my life by the power of the Holy Spirit that is at work in me. Blessed be Your Name Holy Father. Amen.

Further Reading: 1 Corinthians 9: 25.

73. PRAY THAT THE WORD OF GOD WILL GROW MIGHTLY IN YOU

Bible Passage

"So mightily grew the word of God and prevailed" Acts 19: 20.

Precious Father, I thank You, for Your Word is growing mightily in my spirit. In every facet of my life, Your Word is prevailing and producing fruits of righteousness by the power of the Holy Spirit. My spirit is a fertile ground for Your Word to grow and produce lasting results. I declare that I am making tremendous progress from Your Word, and it is seen by all. I thank You, Father, in Jesus' Name. Amen.

Further Reading: Acts 12: 24.

74. THANK GOD FOR THE IMPACTS OF HIS WORD IN YOUR LIFE AND MINISTRY

Bible Passage

"Therefore, get rid of all moral filth and the evil that is so prevalent and humbly accept the word planted in you, which can save you" James 1: 21.

Glorious Father, I thank You profusely from the bottom of my heart for the great and effective impacts of Your Word in my life and ministry. By the impacts of Your Word, I am shining, and kings and nobles are drawn into the brightness of light. From far and near, men and women seek me to be impacted with Your Word. I am making a great impact in ministry by the working of the Word and the testimonies abound in Jesus' Name. Amen.

Further Reading: Philippians 2: 14 – 16

75. PRAY FOR THE IMPACT OF THE WORD IN YOUR COUNTRY AND AROUND THE WORLD

Bible Passage

"So the word of God continued to spread. The number of disciples in Jerusalem grew rapidly, and a great number of priests became obedient to the faith" Acts 6: 7.

Dear Lord God, I thank You for the impact Your Word is making in my country and around the world. In Habakkuk 2: 14, Your Word says that the whole earth will be filled with the knowledge of the glory of the LORD as the waters cover the sea. I thank You for the knowledge of Your Word that has filled and covered the whole earth; Your Name is glorified in all nations and territories of the earth, in Jesus' Name. Amen.

Further Reading: Matthew 24: 14.

76. PRAY THAT THE WORD OF GOD WILL PENETRATE THE HIGH PLACES OF YOUR COUNTRY: GOVERNMENT QUARTERS AND PALACES

Bible Passage

"When the proconsul saw what had happened, he believed, for he was astonished at the teaching about the Lord" Acts 13: 12.

Precious Father, I thank You because Your Word is penetrating and dominating the high places and quarters of my country, state, region, province and city. I declare that those in government from national and local levels in the country are receiving Your Word with gladness. Their decisions and policies are influenced by Your Word. They are only surrounded by godly people with the right counsel. Their hearts are mantled with Your wisdom to always do the right thing in Jesus' Name. Amen.

Further Reading: Acts 13: 7.

77. PRAY FOR GOD'S GLORY AND BEAUTY

Bible Passage

"In that day, the Lord of hosts will become a beautiful crown and a glorious diadem to the remnant of His people" Isaiah 28: 5.

Precious Father, I thank You for Your overwhelming glory and beauty upon my life. You have graced me with Your glory in my health, marriage, business and job, ministry, and relationships. You have made me a bright and shining light to my world, the light of the world. I thank You because Your beauty is seen in me, and it is attracting kings and nobles to me. I exude Your glory and beauty everywhere I go like a sweet-smelling perfume in Jesus' Name. Amen.

Further Reading: Isaiah 4: 2.

78. PRAY THAT YOU ARE EXERCISING YOUR SPIRIT THROUGH THE WORD OF GOD

Bible Passage

"The Spirit himself bears witness with our spirit that we are children of God" Romans 8: 16.

Father, my spirit has been recreated after You. It seeks after You to bring You glory and praise. As I exercise my spirit in doing Your Word, praying, acting my faith and doing good works, men would see Your handiwork in me. They will praise You because that is what I was created to do. I declare that my spirit is pure, holy, righteous and sanctified by Your Word. It is clean and can only produce things that bring You honor in Jesus' Name. Amen.

Further Reading: Romans 8: 10.

79. PRAY FOR A COMPREHENSIVE UNDERSTANDING OF THE WORD AS YOU STUDY IT DAILY

Bible Passage

"Your hands made me and fashioned me; give me understanding, that I may learn Your commandments" Psalm 119: 73.

Lord God, I thank You for granting me the understanding of Your Word. By Your Spirit, I comprehend Your Word easily as I study and meditate on it. You said through the Psalmist that the entrance of Your Word gives light and understanding to the simple. My heart is flooded with the understanding of Your Word in the Name of Jesus Christ. I declare that I have guidance and direction by Your Word in every facet of my life. Halleluiah!

Further Reading: Luke 24: 45.

80. PRAY THAT YOU WOULD ENJOY YOUR INHERITANCE IN CHRIST BY THE WORD

Bible Passage

"To obtain an inheritance which is imperishable and undefiled and will not fade away, reserved in heaven for you" 1 Peter 1: 4.

I thank You, glorious Father for the inheritances that I have in Christ Jesus. By the eternal life that I have in Christ, I am a partaker of Your divine nature, I am heir of Abraham, a joint heir with the Lord Jesus. Divine health, righteousness, eternal life, justification, wisdom, grace heap upon grace, the Holy Spirit are some of the inheritances I have in Christ. I declare that with the good knowledge of the Word I have in my spirit, I am enjoying all my inheritances in Jesus' Name. Amen.

Further Reading: Colossians 1: 12.

81. PRAY FOR WISDOM AND UNDERSTANDING

Bible Passage

"If any of you lacks wisdom, you should ask God, who gives generously to all without finding fault, and it will be given to you" James 1: 5.

Father God, I thank You for granting me wisdom to deal wisely in the affairs of this life. I thank You because by Your wisdom at work in me, I can handle the challenges brought upon our world by this present 'pandemic'. In the Name of Jesus Christ, I declare that I will never fall victim or be plagued with the virus. The Name of the Lord Jesus Christ is named upon me and my household, and we are sealed from any contaminations. Amen.

Further Reading: 1 Corinthians 1: 30.

82. PRAY TO BE ABLE TO FIGHT THE GOOD FIGHT OF FAITH

Bible Passage

"Fight the good fight of the faith. Take hold of the eternal life to which you were called and about which you made the good confession in the presence of many witnesses" 1 Timothy 6: 12.

Lord, I thank You for Your Word that I have laid up in my spirit. Your Word is the weapon with which I build my faith to fight the good fight. Yes, it is a good fight because You have declared me a conqueror even before the fight starts. Your Word – the Sword of the Spirit is in my mouth, and as I declare it, I make war with it. I pull down every dart and arrow of the enemy in Jesus' Name. Amen.

Further Reading: 2 Corinthians 10: 4.

83. PRAY THAT THE WORD WILL GIVE YOU AN UNDERSTANDING OF THE TIMES

Bible Passage

"Redeeming the time, because the days are evil" Ephesians 5: 16.

Lord God, eternality dwells within You. You are the beginning and the end, the Alpha and Omega. I pray not to be ignorant of the times. As I study Your Word, I will understand the times more, and with the knowledge, I will be able to navigate the times because I know the days are evil. By the Spirit and Word of God, I understand world events; I am able to use Your Word to interpret the times in Jesus' Name. Amen.

Further Reading: Ecclesiastes 3: 11.

84. THANK GOD FOR THE BLESSINGS THE WORD BRINGS

Bible Passage

"The blessing of the LORD enriches, and He adds no sorrow to it"

Heavenly Father, I thank You so much for the blessings Your Word brings. Your Word brings faith, hope, courage, knowledge, understanding, grace and beauty. 2 Timothy 3: 16 – 17 says Your Word is Your breath, and it is useful for teaching, rebuking, correcting and training in righteousness so that the servant of God may be thoroughly equipped for every good work. Your Word brings healing to the sick, comfort to the troubled, beauty for ashes and oil of gladness to those who mourn. Glory be to You, Lord, in Jesus' Name. Amen.

Further Reading: Philippians 4: 19.

85. PRAY THAT YOUR FAITH IN GOD WILL CONTINUE TO GROW BY THE WORD

Bible Passage

"So then faith comes by hearing, and hearing by the word of God" Romans 10: 17.

Lord God, I thank You because faith comes from hearing by Your Word. I pray that as I continually study Your Word and put it to practice, my faith will continue to grow. It will continue to grow strong and produce great and effective results. In the Name of the Lord Jesus Christ, I declare that my faith is producing miracles; I am winning every day as I exercise my faith by the Word in Jesus' Name. Amen.

Further Reading: Galatians 3: 5.

86. THANK GOD BECAUSE THE WORD OF GOD IS PREVAILING IN THE INNER CITIES OF YOUR COUNTRY

Bible Passage:

"He brought me up also out of a horrible pit, out of the miry clay, and set my feet upon a rock, and established my goings" Psalm 40: 2.

Blessed Father, I thank You because Your Word is prevailing in the inner cities of my community, county, province, state, region and country. Your Word is reaching the underworld and bring them salvation, healing, wisdom and deliverance. I declare those enslaved by drugs, alcohol, prostitution, homosexuality, gambling and other forms of crimes are receiving the Word, and they are getting free by the power of the Holy Spirit, in the Name of the Lord Jesus Christ. Amen.

Further Reading: Psalm 18: 30.

87. PRAY THAT THE WORD OF GOD IS GLADLY RECEIVED IN REGIONS THAT ARE HOSTILE TO THE GOSPEL

Bible Passage

"Heaven and earth will pass away, but my words will never pass away" Matthew 24: 35.

Father, You say that the Gospel of the kingdom will be preached in all the nations of the world, and then the end will come. I pray, Father, that those You have earmarked for salvation in the nations of the world will not be denied by hostility, wicked government policies, unreasonable and wicked folks. I pray that the Gospel is gladly received in all the countries in the Middle East, Africa, China, North Korea and all the parts of the world in Jesus' Name. Amen.

Further Reading: Isaiah 40: 8.

88. PRAY THAT THE WORD OF GOD WILL BRING FAITH TO THE SICK TO BE HEALED

Bible Passage

"Come to me, all you who are weary and burdened, and I will give you rest" Matthew 11: 28.

Father, in the Name of the Lord Jesus Christ, I thank You for the healing power that Your Word brings. I pray for sick folks in my sphere of contact and those outside that they will receive faith for their healing through the Word of God that comes to them. The Scripture says that the Word of God is medicine to the flesh. As they receive the Word, faith and healing will come to them, and they will be made whole. Amen.

Further Reading: Psalm 30: 2.

89. THANK GOD BECAUSE HIS WORD IS LIVING AND ACTIVE IN YOUR LIFE: IT IS PRODUCING RESULTS IN YOUR LIFE

Bible Passage

"For the word of God is alive and active. Sharper than any double-edged sword, it penetrates even to dividing soul and spirit, joints and marrow; it judges the thoughts and attitudes of the heart" Hebrews 4: 12.

I thank You, dear Father, because Your Word is living and active in my life. It is sharper than any two-edged sword, it penetrates between the soul and the spirit, joints and narrow, and it can discern the intents of my heart. Like the Psalmist, I have hidden Your Word in my heart that I may not sin against You. I thank You, Lord, because Your Word rules my heart; it dominates the thoughts of my heart and helps me to produce righteous thoughts and deeds in Jesus' Name. Amen.

Further Reading: Luke 11: 28.

90. PRAY THAT THE WORD OF GOD WILL ALWAYS GIVE YOU DIRECTION IN LIFE

Bible Passage

"All Scripture is God-breathed and is useful for teaching, rebuking, correcting and training in righteousness, so that the servant of God may be thoroughly equipped for every good work" 2 Timothy 3: 16 – 17.

Dear Lord God, I thank You because Your Word is right and true. Your word is a lamp for my feet, a light on my path. With Your Word, one will never go astray in life. The entrance of Your Word gives light; it gives illumination and direction. I declare that there is no darkness in my path because the Word of God is my light; it gives me direction. Therefore, I will never stumble or my feet slide in Jesus' Name. Amen.

Further Reading: Psalm 119: 105

91. DECLARE THAT YOU ARE A DOER OF THE WORD AND NOT JUST A HEARER ONLY

Bible Passage

"Do not merely listen to the word, and so deceive yourselves. Do what it says" James 1: 22.

In the Name of the Lord Jesus Christ, I declare that I am a doer of the Word and not just one that hears and does nothing with it. The Word of God is for doing. One cannot get the blessings of the Word only by hearing it but when put into practice. Therefore, I declare that I am a practitioner of the Word of God. The new creation does not only obey the Word, but he is a doer. By the power of the Holy Spirit at work in me, as I put the Word to work, it produces tremendous miracles and testimonies for me. Glory to God!

Further Reading: Luke 11: 28.

92. PRAY THAT THE WORD WOULD KEEP YOU UPRIGHT AND BLAMELESS TILL THE DAY OF THE LORD

Bible Passage

"As for God, his way is perfect: the Lord's word is flawless; he shields all who take refuge in him" Psalm 18: 30.

Dear Heavenly Father, I thank You for the efficacy of Your Word to keep me upright and blameless till the day of Jesus Christ. The Psalmist asked a question in Psalm 119: 9, 'How can a young person stay on the path of purity? The answer Your Spirit gave in the same verse is, '...By living according to Your Word.' I declare that by the Spirit of the Lord, I will continually live according to the Word of God in Jesus' Name. Amen.

Further Reading: Psalm 33: 4.

93. PRAY THAT BY THE SPIRIT YOU WOULD METAMORPHOSE INTO THE IMAGE OF THE WORD OF GOD

Bible Passage

"And we all, who with unveiled faces contemplate the Lord's glory, are being transformed into his image with ever-increasing glory, which comes from the Lord, who is the Spirit." 2 Corinthians 3: 18.

Father, in the Name of the Lord Jesus Christ, I pray that by the Holy Spirit at work in me as I study the Word and meditate on it, I am metamorphosed into the same image as the Word has of me. I am the righteousness of God in Christ Jesus. I am a chosen people, a royal priesthood, a holy nation, God's special possession, and I am declaring the praises of God who called me out of darkness into His wonderful light. Blessed be God!

Further Reading: James 1: 23 – 24.

94. THANK GOD BECAUSE HIS WORD IS MATURING YOU INTO A PERFECT PERSON

Bible Passage

"Like newborn infants, long for the pure spiritual milk, that by it you may grow up into salvation" 1 Peter 2: 2.

Father, I thank You for the maturing of Your Word. I am commanded to Your Word that is able to mature me and give me my inheritance amongst them that are sanctified. I desire the sincere milk of the Word of God that I may grow by it. Lord, with Your Word, my words are seasoned with grace; my actions are befitting of a Christian. My ways are perfected by the Word of God in my spirit in Jesus' Name. Amen.

Further Reading: 1 Corinthians 13: 11.

95. THANK GOD FOR THE CLEANSING OF HIS WORD IN YOUR LIFE

Bible Passage

"How can a young person stay on the path of purity? By living according to your word" Psalm 119: 9.

I thank You, Most Holy Father, for the cleansing power of Your Word. Your Word has the efficacy to cleanse me of every guilt and condemnation. Dear Lord Jesus, You said in Scriptures, 'You are already clean because of the word which I have spoken to you.' This is my testimony. I am cleansed by the Word of God in my spirit by the power of the Holy Spirit, in the Name of the Lord Jesus Christ.

Further Reading: Psalm 30: 18.

96. PRAY FOR FULFILLMENT

Bible Passage:

"You will lay your gold in the dust, and the gold of Ophir among the stones of the brooks. Yes, the Almighty will be your gold and your precious silver; for then you will have your delight in the Almighty, and lift up your face to God. You will make your prayer to Him, He will hear you, and you will pay your vows. You will also declare a thing, and it will be established for you; so light will shine on your ways. When they cast you down and you say, 'Exaltation will come!' Then He will save the humble person. Job 22: 24-29 (NKJV)"

I know it is your will, O Lord, to bring me into my season of fulfillment. I receive all that you have prepared for me in eternity to progress and prosper in your plans and purpose for my life. I reject every spirit of stagnation and backwardness in my life, business, and family today. I declare that my time of fulfillment and breakthrough is here. I refuse to condescend to mediocrity or stay in the valley of obscurity. This is my new dawn; I will rise and shine in the glory of my God in Jesus' Name, amen.

Further reading: Ezekiel 12: 28, Philippians 1: 6

97. PRAY FOR SANCTIFICATION

Bible Passage

"By which will we are sanctified through the offering of the body of Jesus Christ once for all" Hebrews 10: 10.

Heavenly Father, I thank You for sanctifying me, making me holy and fit for Your use. I reject every sense of condemnation. The Lord Jesus Christ has paid for my guilt and declared me holy and sanctified. No devil can fill my heart with guilt anymore because I am alive unto God. I am the righteousness of God in Christ Jesus. Glory to God, sin has no hold on me again. I am thorough washed and meet for the Master's honor. I thank You, Father, in Jesus' Name. Amen.

Further Reading: 1 Corinthians 6: 11.

98. PRAY FOR INCREASE FAITH

Bible Passage

"For in the gospel the righteousness of God is revealed—a righteousness that is by faith from first to last, just as it is written: "The righteous will live by faith" Romans 1: 17.

Lord God, I recognize that I must increase my faith daily. I pray for increased faith in every area of my life. Your Word says You dealt everyone a measure of faith. It is my responsibility to increase my faith. Thus, I declare that my heart is filled with increased faith as I give myself to the study of Your Word. I have the God-kind of faith, faith that can move mountains in the Name of the Lord Jesus Christ. Amen.

Further Reading: Matthew 21: 22.

Chapter 5: PRAYER FOR DIVINE HEALING

The Word of God says that healing is the children's bread. In other words, it is God's desire for you to be well; for you to be healed of that sickness and live in divine health. It is the lie of the devil for you to think that God will not heal you or that God uses sickness to punish or humble His children. No, God does not do that. He does not use the instrument of the devil to punish His children. Remember what the Word says, 'how God anointed the Lord Jesus Christ with the Holy Spirit and power, who went about doing good. He went about healing those who were sick and afflicted of the devil, for God was with Him. If it was God that afflicted His children with sickness or use infirmity and diseases to humble His children, how would He also send Jesus to heal them of the sicknesses?

You can see that God wants you well. He wants you to live in divine health perpetually. So when you say the prayers in this category, believe that God wants you well and He will heal you if you are sick or anyone you want healed. By the stripes of the Lord Jesus Christ, He healed you already. As you say these prayers, you are activating that healing; stirring it alive in your health and life. Do not allow the devil or your conscience inhibit your healing because God delights in your health.

99. PRAYER FOR HEALING

Bible Passage

"But if the Spirit of Him who raised Jesus from the dead dwells in you, He who raised Christ from the dead will also give life to your mortal bodies through His Spirit who dwells in you" Romans 8: 11.

Dear Father, I thank You because Your Spirit dwells in me and vitalizes my physical body. Therefore, no sickness, disease or infirmity can successfully inhabit my body. I rebuke sickness, disease and death in my body. I declare that I do not consider symptoms because they are lying vanities; I live divine health always because this is my heritage in Christ Jesus. Divine health is mine! Every infirmity that hitherto existed in my members is totally healed by the power of the Holy Spirit that lives in me in Jesus' Name. Amen.

Further Reading: John 5: 21.

100. PRAY FOR THE DIVINE HEALING POWER OF GOD ON SICK CHILDREN IN HOSPITALS IN YOUR COUNTRY

Bible Passage

"Behold, I will bring to it health and healing, and I will heal them; and I will reveal to them an abundance of peace and truth" Jeremiah 33: 6.

Blessed Father, I thank You for the life and health of precious children who are sick in hospital beds. Lord God, I know You love them and would want them living in sound health. Thus, I pray for their healing. In the Name of the Lord Jesus Christ, I declare that the doctors and nurses know what to do in each of their cases. I declare them healed of whatever infirmities afflict them. Their health is restored in Jesus' Name. Amen.

Further Reading: Jeremiah 30: 17a.

101. PRAY TO HEAL YOUR FAMILY MEMBERS THAT ARE SICK

Bible Passage

"He sent His word and healed them, and delivered them from their destructions" Psalm 107: 20.

Father God, in the precious Name of the Lord Jesus Christ, I pray for any of my family members who are sick. I restore them to sound health; I declare them whole by the power of the Holy Spirit. You foul spirit of darkness responsible for ailing conditions, I charge you to depart from them and return no more. They are free from the oppression of the enemy. I declare that they live in perpetual sound health. Amen.

Further Reading: Jeremiah 17: 14.

102. PRAY FOR MEMBERS OF YOUR LOCAL ASSEMBLY THAT ARE SICK; PRONOUNCE GOD'S HEALING UPON THEM

Bible Passage

"Is anyone among you sick? Then he must call for the elders of the church and they are to pray over him, anointing him with oil in the name of the Lord" James 5: 14.

Kind Heavenly Father, You said in Your Word that 'You desire for us to prosper and live in sound health even as our souls prosper. I thank You because Your desire comes to pass in the lives of members of my local assembly that are sick. I declare that healing is their bread. They are made every whit whole in their bodies, souls and spirits. I declare that the Word of God comes alive in their health by the power of the Holy Spirit. I thank You, dear Father, in Jesus' Name. Amen.

Further Reading: Psalm 41: 4.

103. PRAY FOR THE HEALING TOUCH OF GOD ON MINISTERS OF THE GOSPEL THAT ARE SICK

Bible Passage

"But for you who fear My name, the sun of righteousness will rise with healing in its wings; and you will go forth and skip about like calves from the stall" Malachi 4: 2.

Holy Father, I thank You for the lives and health of Your ministers. I pray for those that are sick with one infirmity or another. I declare them healed by the power of the Spirit of God in their spirits. They are God's channels of faith and healing to their congregations. Thus, I pray they are restored to sound health in Jesus' Name. I pray that the same anointing that they use to minister health and healing to their flocks work for them. Their faith is stirred to use the Name of Jesus Christ to walk in divine health. Halleluiah! Amen.

Further Reading: Jeremiah 8: 22.

104. PRAY FOR PREGNANT WOMEN WHOSE LIVES AND PREGNANCIES ARE BEING THREATENED BY SICKNESS: DECLARE THEM HEALED

Bible Passage

"And the midwives said to Pharaoh, "Because the Hebrew women are not like the Egyptian women; for they are lively and give birth before the midwives come to them" Exodus 1: 19.

Lord God, You are the Father of glory and mercy. I thank You for the lives and pregnancies of these Christian women that an enemy is threatening with sicknesses. I pray for Your divine intervention in their cases. I declare them strengthened and strong. They are able to carry their pregnancies to term in Jesus' Name. The plans of the devil and his cohorts are brought to nought in their lives in Jesus' Name. Amen.

Further Reading: Matthew 15: 28.

105. CALL FORTH HEALING FOR CHRISTIANS THAT ARE CRITICALLY SICK IN HOSPITALS IN YOUR COUNTRY

Bible Passage

"*The Lord will sustain him upon his sickbed; in his illness, You restore him to health*" Psalm 41: 3.

In the matchless Name of the Lord Jesus Christ, I call forth the divine healing of God on Christians that are critically ill. Whether they are in a hospital or at home, I declare them healed. The power of God's Spirit overwhelms them right now, and their faith is stirred to receive their healing in Jesus' Name. Father, I pray for forgiveness of sins for those who are sick as a result of their sins. I declare that the Name of the Lord Jesus is named upon them, and they abound in God's divine health. Amen.

Further Reading: Hosea 6: 1.

106. PRAY FOR FRONTLINE HEALTH WORKERS THAT ARE SICK WITH COVID OR OTHER SICKNESSES: HEAL THEM IN THE NAME OF JESUS

Bible Passage

"Heal the sick, raise the dead, cleanse the lepers, drive out demons. Freely you have received; freely give" Matthew 10: 8.

Precious Father, blessed be Your Holy Name. I pray for frontline health workers who are sick with Covid-19 or any other sicknesses. I heal them in the Name of Jesus Christ. I pray that their faith is strong and that they are not in any way discouraged by the so-called 'pandemic'. I pray that they and their families are continually protected by the power of the Holy Spirit. I thank You, Lord God, for their lives in Jesus' Name. Amen.

Further Reading: Acts 3: 6.

107. PRAY FOR YOURSELF; DECLARE THAT YOU CONTINUALLY ENJOY SOUND HEALTH

Bible Passage

"Beloved, I pray that you may prosper in all things and be in health, just as your soul prospers" 1 John 3: 2.

Dear Lord God, I thank You for the sound health I enjoy. You said it is Your desire that I prosper and enjoy good health even as my spiritual life prospers. In the Name of the Lord Jesus Christ, I declare that I continually enjoy divine health. That same Spirit that raised Jesus from the dead resides in me; He vitalizes my mortal body. The Holy Spirit perambulates my body to keep it healthy in Jesus' Name. Amen.

Further Reading: Malachi 4: 2.

108. PRAY FOR THOSE WHO ARE SICK IN THE HOSPITALS THAT DOCTORS HAVE GIVEN UP ON: RESTORE THEIR HEALTH IN THE NAME OF JESUS

Bible Passage

"The Lord will sustain him upon his sickbed; in his illness, You restore him to health" Psalm 41: 3.

Glorious Father, I thank You because there is nothing impossible for someone who has faith. I pray for the restoration of the health of folks critically ill in the hospital, and the doctors can no longer help. Lord, I restore their health in the mighty Name of Jesus. Miraculously, they are responding to treatments and walking out of the hospital whole. The Name of Jesus Christ is powerful and higher than any sickness. Thus, I rebuke every sickness the devil has used to afflict these ones in Jesus' Name. Amen.

Further Reading: 2 Kings 20: 5.

109. PRAY FOR THOSE SUFFERING FROM INCURABLE SICKNESSES: USE THE NAME OF JESUS TO HEAL THEM

Bible Passage

"And he called to him his twelve disciples and gave them authority over unclean spirits, to cast them out, and to heal every disease and every affliction." Matthew 10: 1.

Lord God, I pray specifically for those whose ailments do not have a cure except for a miracle, such as diabetes, cancer, high blood pressure, etc. I have seen several healing miracles where people have been healed from these sicknesses, so I know You are the only One that can help these folks. Therefore, I declare them healed; they are free to serve God in good health. I pronounce them totally healed by the power of the Holy Spirit in Jesus' Name. Amen.

Further Reading: 1 Peter 2: 24

110. PRAY FOR THE ELDERLY THAT ARE SICK; PRONOUNCE THEM STRENGTHENED AND HEALED

Bible Passage

"He heals the brokenhearted and binds up their wounds" Psalm 147: 3.

Father God, I pray for the elderly that are lying in hospitals and homes sick. I pronounce them strengthened and healed. You are the ancient of days, the beginning and the end. Eternity lies within Your palms and healings are under Your wings. Thus, I pray that You have compassion for these elderly men and women. A lot of them are in that condition as a result of how wrong they have lived their lives. Lord, I thank You for Your mercy upon them. I declare them healed in Jesus' Name. Amen.

Further Reading: Psalm 103: 2 – 3.

111. PRAY FOR THOSE THAT WORK IN THE HEALTH SECTOR: DECLARE THAT THEY ARE GUIDED BY GOD'S WISDOM

Bible Passage

"May the favor of the Lord our God rest upon us; establish for us the work of our hands—yes, establish the work of our hands" Psalm 90: 17.

Father, I thank You for our beloved health sector workers. I pray that they are guided by Your wisdom. Their hearts and minds are mantled with Your fear, and they refuse to be manipulated or misguided to do the wrong things. Their hearts are filled with compassion and love for those they care for. For all their righteous and sincere intents, the Lord will establish for them in Jesus' Name. They will deal wisely, conscious of their oath and commitment to humanity. Halleluiah!

Further Reading: Psalm 37: 23.

112. PRAY FOR THOSE THAT MAKE INVESTMENTS IN THE HEALTH SECTOR THAT THEY WOULD DO THEIR BUSINESSES WITH THE FEAR OF GOD

Bible Passage

"For kings and for all that are in authority; that we may lead a quiet and peaceable life in all godliness and honesty" 1 Timothy 2: 2.

Blessed Heavenly Father, I thank You for those that make business investments in the health sector, those at the international, national and local levels. I declare that they will make their investments with the fear of God. I pray for wisdom for them. They will know the right thing to do at the right time. By the power of the Holy Spirit, I declare that they will know how to resist every attempt to be manipulated to mislead the world in Jesus' Name. Amen.

Further Reading: Proverbs 9: 10.

113. PRAY FOR THOSE SUFFERING FROM HEALTH PROBLEMS AS A RESULT OF THE OUTBREAK OF DISEASES

Bible Passage

"How God anointed Jesus of Nazareth with the Holy Spirit and with power. He went about doing good and healing all who were oppressed by the devil, for God was with him" Acts 10: 38.

Heavenly Father, in the Name of the Lord Jesus Christ, I pray for those who are suffering health challenges as a result of an outbreak of diseases in parts of the world. I declare a stop to the outbreak of diseases, and I pronounce divine healing for those affected. The Name of Jesus Christ is higher than whatever the disease or infection is called. The diseases are decimated, and the people are made whole by the power of the Holy Spirit. Amen.

Further Reading: Luke 9: 1.

114. DECLARE THAT ANY SICK PERSON YOU LAY YOUR HANDS ON WILL RECEIVE HEALING

Bible Passage

"They will pick up serpents, and if they drink any deadly poison, it will not hurt them; they will lay hands on the sick, and they will recover" Mark 16: 18.

Dear Lord Jesus, You said in Your Word that I would lay hands on the sick, and they will recover. By the authority I have in You and the power to use Your Name, I declare that anyone sick who has faith to be healed will receive healing when I lay hands on them. I declare that virtue will proceed from me through my hands, and whatever the ailment is will be healed instantly, and devils will check on those they possessed by the power of the Holy Spirit. Amen.

Further Reading: Acts 28: 8.

115. DECLARE THAT YOU HAVE PASSED FROM DEATH TO LIFE; SICKNESS DOES NOT HAVE DOMINION OVER YOU AGAIN

Bible Passage

"We know that we have passed from death to life, because we love the brethren. He who does not love his brother abides in death" 1John 3: 14.

Glory to God in the Highest! I declare in the Name of the Lord Jesus Christ that I have passed from death to life. I was dead in Christ once, and I die no more. The life that I live now is not subject to sicknesses, diseases, informalities, depression, death or the devil. I live the same life of God – eternal life, and it is not susceptible to sickness, death or the devil. I do not die, and nothing of mine dies because my life is hidden in Christ in God. I thank You, Father, for this privilege in Jesus' Name. Amen.

Further Reading: John 5: 24.

116. PRAY FOR MEDICAL WORKERS: THAT THEY WOULD ATTEND TO THEIR PATIENTS WITH DUE DILIGENCE, FAITH AND THE FEAR OF GOD

Bible Passage

"The LORD is near to the brokenhearted; He saves the contrite in spirit" Psalm 34: 18.

Father, I pray for medical workers, especially doctors, nurses, medical laboratory scientists, Paramedics and pharmacists. I pray that they continually understand how important their duties are in trying to save lives. I pray that by the Spirit of God, they will know how to manage their emotions, especially when they are feeling overwhelmed. I pray that they would not be callous but carry out their duties with due diligence, faith and the fear of God in Jesus' Name. Amen.

Further Reading: Psalm 147: 3.

117. PRAY FOR CANCER PATIENTS AND THOSE WITH OTHER TERMINAL DISEASES: DECLARE THAT THE NAME OF JESUS IS SUPERIOR TO ANY SICKNESS

Bible Passage

"And on the banks, on both sides of the river, there will grow all kinds of trees for food. Their leaves will not wither, nor their fruit fail, but they will bear fresh fruit every month, because the water for them flows from the sanctuary. Their fruit will be for food and their leaves for healing" Ezekiel 47: 12.

Father God, I pray for folks suffering from cancer and other terminal diseases. I declare that the Name of Jesus Christ is superior to their sicknesses. I declare them healed by the authority I have in Christ and in His mighty Name. Even as they breathe in right now, they inhale healing into their systems. I cleanse their bodies, blood, cells, bones, nerves and brain of every affliction. The Name of Jesus reigns supreme in their bodies and health by the power of the Holy Spirit. Amen.

Further Reading: Revelation 22: 2.

118. INTERCESSION FOR THE SICK AND THOSE AFFECTED BY THE VIRUS

Bible Passage

"Is any sick among you? let him call for the elders of the church; and let them pray over him, anointing him with oil in the name of the Lord: And the prayer of faith shall save the sick, and the Lord shall raise him up; and if he have committed sins, they shall be forgiven him" James 5: 14 – 16.

Father, I pray for the sick in my family and sphere of contact, especially those infected by Covid-19. I declared them healed in the Name of Jesus. The Word of God says that everything that has a name in heaven, on earth and underneath the earth is subject to the Name of Jesus. Therefore, I rebuke the spirit responsible for the spread of this coronavirus. I command it to stop in its track, and the people are healed and free in Jesus' Name. Amen.

Further Reading: Mark 11: 24.

119. PRAY FOR THE FAMILY OF THOSE WHOSE LOVE ONES DIED OF COVID-19

Bible Passage

"Blessed are those who mourn, for they shall be comforted" Matthew 5: 4.

Father, in the Name of the Lord Jesus Christ, I pray for the family whose loved ones died as a result of Covid-19, and I pray that they are comforted with Your peace. I pray that help comes to them from You directly so that they will know that You are still with them. I pray that their hearts are strong; the devil will not find space to take undue advantage of them. Halleluiah!

Further Reading: 2 Corinthians 1: 3 – 4.

120. PRAY FOR INCREASED ACTIVITIES OF HEALING ANGELS IN AND AROUND YOUR HOME AND CHURCH

Bible Passage

"Are they not all ministering spirits sent forth to serve those who will inherit salvation?" Hebrews 1: 14.

Lord, You said through the Prophet Isaiah that 'And no resident of Zion will say, "I am sick." The people who dwell there will be forgiven of iniquity.' Therefore, I pray for the increased activities of healing and health angels in and around my home and Church in Jesus' Name. I pray that my faith and all those around me will soar; our faith is activated to enjoy our health. Our ministry angels protect us and grant us healings in Jesus' Name. Amen.

Further Reading: Psalm 91: 11.

121. PRAY FOR HEALING FOR COUNTRIES THAT ARE AFFLICTED BY COVID-19: DISPATCH HEALING ANGELS TO HEAL THEM

Bible Passage

"Then the devil left Him, and behold, angels came and ministered to Him" Matthew 4: 11.

Father God, I pray for countries and regions of the world still being ravaged by Covid-19. I dispatch healing angels to their rescue in Jesus' Name. I pray that the Christians wake up to their responsibility to pray and stand in the gap for their nations and peoples. Lord God, as these Christians pray, please hear them and heal their land. Restore health, hope, peace and prosperity to them. I put a stop to the activities of the demons responsible for Covid-19 all over the world in Jesus' Name. Amen.

Further Reading: Luke 22: 43.

122. PRAY FOR FRONTLINE HEALTH WORKERS

Bible Passage

"*Is there no balm in Gilead? Is there no physician there? Why then is there no healing for the wound of my people?*" Jeremiah 8: 22.

Father, I thank You for our frontline health workers who have had to take great risks in the face of this pandemic. I pray that they are protected from being infected by this virus. Those who are already affected, I declare that Your healing rests on them. I pray that their hearts are filled with wisdom, courage and faith. They know how to handle every infected and sick patient. I declare that they do the right thing at the right time, in Jesus' Name. Amen.

Further Reading: Matthew 9: 12.

123. PRAY FOR GOVERNMENT OFFICIALS AND HEALTH POLICYMAKERS

Bible Passage

"First of all, then, I urge that petitions, prayers, intercessions, and thanksgiving be offered for everyone— for kings and all those in authority, that we may live peaceful and quiet lives in all godliness and holiness" 1 Timothy 2: 1 – 2.

Precious Father, I pray for our government and all those in positions of authority. I pray Your wisdom guides them, that their policies reflect Your will for humanity. I pray that they are protected from unreasonable and wicked influences that seek to manipulate them against Your Word. I pray that they will always rule with Your fear in their heart so that we may live peaceful and quiet lives in all godliness and holiness in Jesus' Name. Amen.

Further Reading: Romans 13: 1.

124. PRAY FOR TOTAL RESTORATION

Bible Passage

"But I will restore you to health and heal your wounds,' declares the LORD, 'because you are called an outcast, Zion for whom no one cares" Jeremiah 30: 17.

Father, I thank You for my life and for those very close to me. I thank You for sparing our lives in this period of the Covid outbreak. I pray for total restoration for my family and me and for my friends as well. I pray that everything we have lost is restored to us by the power of the Holy Spirit. In Jesus' Name, I declare that like Job, all that we lose are restored to us more than a hundredfold. Amen.

Further Reading: Malachi 4: 2.

Chapter 6: PRAYER FOR PROSPERITY & BUSINESSES

There are those who believe and preach that to be prosperous is carnality. This is a big lie from the pit of hell. The Apostle John by the Spirit lets us know that God desires us to prosper and be in sound health, even as our souls prosper. The Word of God says in Deuteronomy 8: 18 that it is God who has given us the power to make wealth. The Psalmist also lets us know that it is God that prospers us; He delights in our prosperity (Psalm 35: 27). Remember the patriarchs Abraham, Isaac, Jacob, David, Solomon and co. They were very wealthy, and God was the source of their long-lasting prosperity, the same God who has blessed you with all that pertains to life and godliness.

The opportunity for you to pray for prosperity and business is an opportunity for you to cause all circumstances to work for your good. As Christians, remember, we play by a different set of rules. We do not play like the rest of the world. In the place of prayer, you cause the forces of prosperity to work for you. The prayers in this group are meant to stir faith in your heart to cause you to prosper and enjoy God's blessing upon your business. As you pray, expect miracles; expect a complete turnaround in your business. You will see the Hand of God so strong, causing people and situations to align in your favor. Remember that He delights in your prosperity.

125. THANK GOD FOR BLESSING YOU WITH ALL YOU REQUIRE TO LIVE THE GOOD LIFE

Bible Passage

"Accordingly, His divine power has given us all things toward life and godliness, through the knowledge of the One having called us by His own glory and excellence" 2 Peter 1: 3.

Precious Father, in the Name of the Lord Jesus Christ, I thank You profusely from my heart for blessing me with all I require to live the good life. I am blessed with the corn and wine of Jacob; thus, I do not lack food or anything good. You have blessed and anointed my mind with great and lofty ideas to make the best out of life. I am blessed on all sides, and I have become a blessing to my world. Glory to God!

Further Reading: 2 Thessalonians 2: 14.

126. DECLARE THAT YOU ARE NOT POOR BUT SUPER RICH

Bible Passage

"For you know the grace of our Lord Jesus Christ, that though He was rich, yet for your sakes He became poor, that you through His poverty might become rich" 2 Corinthians 8: 9.

In the Name of the Lord Jesus Christ, I declare that I am rich. The Lord Jesus Christ became poor so that through His poverty, I may become rich. Therefore, I declare I am rich in substance. I am rich in gold, silver, corn, wine, a flock of sheep and cattle. I am wealthy in Euros, Pounds, Dollars and every major currency in the world. I am a creator of wealth from the power of the Holy Spirit at work in me. Amen.

Further Reading: Genesis 13: 2.

127. PRAY FOR YOUR BUSINESS OR JOB: DECLARE THAT YOU PROSPER IN IT

Bible Passage

"Then the LORD your God will make you most prosperous in all the work of your hands and in the fruit of your womb, the young of your livestock and the crops of your land. The LORD will again delight in you and make you prosperous, just as he delighted in your ancestors" Deuteronomy 30: 9.

The Word of God says I will prosper in all that I put my hand to do. Based on this premise, I declare that my job and businesses prosper. The mighty Hand of God is strong on all that I do to make money because my finances are for Kingdom advancement. I do not take decisions that will bring me losses; rather, I always make a profit. In the Name of the Lord Jesus Christ, I deal wisely in all my business dealings. I make progress by the Spirit of God in me. Praise God!

Further Reading: Genesis 13: 5 – 6.

128. PRAY FOR THE OUTPOURING OF GOD'S BLESSINGS

Bible Passage

"Blessed be the God and Father of our Lord Jesus Christ, who has blessed us in Christ with every spiritual blessing in the heavenly places, even as he chose us in him before the foundation of the world, that we should be holy and blameless before him" Ephesians 1: 3 – 4.

I thank You, gracious Father, for the outpouring of Your blessings on me in Jesus' Name. You have blessed us with all that pertains to life and godliness. Therefore, I declare that I will never lack anything. I am Your channel of blessing to my world of contact. Anyone that has contact with me is automatically blessed to be a blessing. I declare that I am blessed in my going out and in my coming in. Praise God!

Further Reading: Deuteronomy 28: 2.

129. DECLARE THAT YOU ARE ABOVE THE ECONOMIC SYSTEMS OF THE WORLD

Bible Passage

"Seeing that Abraham shall surely become a great and mighty nation and all the nations of the earth shall be blessed in him?" Genesis 18: 18.

In the name of Jesus Christ, I declare that I live above the economic systems of the world. I cannot be affected by inflation or economic meltdown. Job 22: 29 says, 'When men are cast down, then thou shall say, There is lifting up, and he shall save the humble person.' I declare I can never be cast down because I am above only. I am perpetually lifted by the power of the Holy Spirit at work in me. Praise God!

Further Reading: Genesis 22: 18

130. DECLARE THAT YOU AND YOUR BUSINESS DO NOT KNOW WHEN HEAT COMES

Bible Passage

"For he shall be like a tree planted by the waters, Which spreads out its roots by the river, And will not fear when heat comes; But its leaf will be green, And will not be anxious in the year of drought, Nor will cease from yielding fruit" Jeremiah 17: 8.

In the name of Jesus Christ of Nazareth, I declare that I am like a tree planted by the water. I spread out my roots by the river, and I do not know when the heat comes. My leaves are evergreen! I refuse to be anxious in the year or times of drought, economic meltdown, recession, etc. I produce fruits that abide in all seasons by the power of the Holy Spirit at work in me. Glory to God!

Further Reading: Job 29: 19.

131. PRAY FOR STRENGTH

Bible Passage

"I can do all things through him who strengthens me" Philippians 4: 13.

Precious Father, I thank You for granting me Your strength by the Holy Spirit. I can do all things through Your Spirit that strengthens me. In the name of the Lord Jesus Christ, I declare that I am strong in the Lord and in the strength of His might. My strength is daily renewed so that when I run, I do not grow weary, and when I walk, I do not faint. The Lord is my strength. Halleluiah!

Further Reading: Ephesians 6: 10.

132. DECLARE THAT YOU MAKE WISE BUSINESS DECISIONS: YOU DO NOT SUFFER WHAT THE WORLD SUFFERS

Bible Passage

"But if any of you lacks wisdom, let him ask of God, who gives to all generously and without reproach, and it will be given to him" James 1: 5.

Glory to God in the Highest! I declare in the name of the Lord Jesus Christ that I deal wisely in all my business decisions. My decisions, choices and actions are led by the Holy Spirit. Thus, I do not take decisions like the world does, nor do I suffer what the world suffers. The wisdom of God is functioning in me always, especially as I meditate on the Word of God daily. I do the right thing the first time and in the right way. Blessed be God!

Further Reading: James 3: 17.

133. PROPHECY AND CALL FORTH BIG BUSINESSES, CONTRACTS AND OPPORTUNITIES

Bible Passage

"Therefore I tell you, whatever you ask for in prayer, believe that you have received it, and it will be yours" Mark 11: 24.

I thank You, God, for the gift of life and for the ability I have to chart the course of my life with my prophecies and faith-filled words. In the name of the Lord Jesus, I declare that I receive big businesses, contracts and awesome opportunities to make good money.

I receive the right information for big businesses by the power of the Holy Spirit. Men and women seek me out to do me good. My quotations are preferred because they are anointed of the Holy Spirit. Halleluiah!

Further Reading: Matthew 7: 7.

134. DECLARE THAT YOUR PROSPERITY IS FOR KINGDOM ADVANCEMENT

Bible Passage

"And you shall remember the LORD your God, for it is He who gives you power to get wealth, that He may establish His covenant which He swore to your fathers, as it is this day" Deuteronomy 8: 18.

Lord God, I thank You for giving me the power to make wealth. I declare that my prosperity is for the advancement of the Kingdom of God here on earth. I am a kingdom financier! I sponsor the Gospel, ensuring it goes around the whole world so that men would be saved. I declare that I am a partner with God in ensuring that souls are snatched out of the Kingdom of darkness into the Kingdom of light, the Kingdom of God's dear Son, Jesus Christ. Glory to God! Amen.

Further Reading: Proverbs 10: 22.

135. DECLARE THAT YOUR JOB OR BUSINESS IS A VEHICLE TO REACH YOUR WORLD FOR JESUS

Bible Passage

"Then the Spirit said to Philip, "Go up and join this chariot" Acts 8: 29.

Father God, in the Name of Jesus Christ, I declare that my job or business is a vehicle for me to reach my world for the Lord Jesus Christ. My passion for spreading the good news of Christ's salvation inspires me to reach all those I do business with the Gospel. I declare that I am first a Christian before a business or career person. Everybody that comes in contact with me comes in contact with the Gospel by the power of the Holy Spirit at work in me. Amen.

Further Reading: Acts 18: 3.

136. DECLARE THAT YOUR FINANCES DO NOT SUFFER INFLATION BUT RETAIN THEIR VALUE BY THE SPIRIT OF GOD

Bible Passage

"Then Isaac sowed in that land, and reaped in the same year a hundredfold; and the LORD blessed him" Genesis 26: 12.

I am not of this world, nor do my finances belong here. In the name of the Lord Jesus Christ, my money cannot suffer inflation or devaluation. By the power of the Holy Spirit, my money retains its value because I pay my tithe, and I am a Gospel financier. Every devourer is rebuked for my sake in the Name of Jesus. My finances are anointed; they can buy anything with good value. My money is money on a mission for the Kingdom of God. Amen.

Further Reading: Genesis 24: 1.

137. PRAY AGAINST WRONG GOVERNMENT POLICIES THAT CRUMBLE BUSINESSES OR CAUSE JOB LOSSES

Bible Passage

"Devise your strategy, but it will be thwarted; propose your plan, but it will not stand, for God is with us" Isaiah 8: 10.

Blessed Father, Your Word says the heart of the king is in Your Hands, and You turn it the direction You please. In the Name of Jesus Christ, I pray against wrong government policies that crumble businesses or cause job losses. I pray that our policymakers are always rightly advised; they are led by the Spirit of God in the decisions they make. Every wrong counsel is frustrated. I declare that my job or business is secure in the Name of Jesus Christ.

Further Reading: Job 5: 12.

138. PRAY AGAINST FRAUDSTERS: PEOPLE THAT COME TO YOU SUBTLE BUT WITH THE INTENTION TO DEFRAUD YOU

Bible Passage

"Woe to those who plan iniquity, to those who plot evil on their beds! At morning's light they carry it out because it is in their power to do it. They covet fields and seize them, and houses, and take them. They defraud people of their homes; they rob them of their inheritance" Micah 2: 1 – 2.

Precious Father, I thank You for the Spirit of wisdom that I have in me. I declare that I will always function with the wisdom of God. I rebuke every manipulation of fraudsters to defraud me. In whatever means they might come, they will stumble and fall. My businesses, bank account, and business portfolios are secured in Jesus' Name. I am able to recognize any intentions to defraud me in person, through the internet, through recommendations or whatever means in Jesus' Name. Amen.

Further Reading: Psalm 36: 4.

139. PRAY FOR THE ECONOMY OF YOUR COUNTRY, DECLARE THAT IT CAN ONLY BE A BLESSING TO YOU

Bible Passage

"*If you are willing and obedient, you will eat the good things of the land*" Isaiah 1: 19.

Father God, I thank You for the economy of my country. I pray that it will continue to improve from glory to glory. I pronounce growth and development over the economy by the power of the Holy Spirit. I pray that the economy will only experience growth and development in every sector of our national life. Those who manage our economy will know the right steps to take at every time to bring prosperity to our country in Jesus' Name. Amen.

Further Reading: Job 36: 11.

140. PRAY FOR CHRISTIANS IN BUSINESS: DECLARE THAT THEY MAKE PROGRESS BY THE SPIRIT OF GOD

Bible Passage

"And He said to me, "My grace is sufficient for you, for My strength is made perfect in weakness." Therefore most gladly I will rather boast in my infirmities, that the power of Christ may rest upon me" 2 Corinthians 12: 9.

Father, in the Name of the Lord Jesus Christ, I pray for Christians in business; I pray that they will continually make progress in their businesses with the help of the Holy Spirit. In all that they do, they make supernatural progress; they advance by the Spirit of God. I declare that they are the best at what they do. In every sector, Christian businesses and business owners are on top. The best belongs to the children of God. Halleluiah!

Further Reading: 1 Corinthians 2: 5.

141. MORE MONEY IN THE HANDS OF CHRISTIANS IS THE PROSPERITY OF THE CHURCH. DECLARE THAT CHRISTIANS WILL CONTINUE TO PROSPER IN ALL THEY DO

Bible Passage

"*I can do all things through Christ who gives me strength*" Philippians 4: 13.

In the Name of the Lord Jesus Christ, I declare that Christians will continually prosper in all that they do. They are favored by God, and it translates earthly blessings. I declare that Christians are bold to initiate great business ideas and can bring them to fruition. I declare the biggest enterprises and corporations in the world are owned by Christians, and they use these opportunities to advance the Gospel all around the world to the praise and glory of God. Amen.

Further Reading: 2 Corinthians 3: 5 – 6.

142. DECLARE Prosperity AND RECOVERY OF BUSINESSES AFTER COVID-19

Bible Passage

"You will also decree a thing, and it will be established for you; and light will shine on your ways" Job 22: 28.

Father, I thank You for fast recoveries and prosperity of businesses after the deceptions of Covid-19. I pray for business owners that have suffered great losses to be bold to start all over. I pray that they are strengthened; they know they need to take the right steps to come back afloat in Jesus' Name. Like Job, I pray that their latter times will be far better than how they were before. By the Spirit of God, their businesses recover and prosper effortlessly in Jesus' Name. Amen.

Further Reading: Lamentation 3: 37.

143. DECLARE THAT THE ECONOMY MANAGERS OF YOUR COUNTRY DEAL WITH THE WISDOM OF GOD AND NOT SELFISHNESS

Bible Passage:

"Do nothing out of selfish ambition or vain conceit. Rather, in humility value others above yourselves" Philippians 2: 3.

In the Name of the Lord Jesus Christ, I declare that our national economy managers do their jobs with the wisdom of God and not selfishness. I pray that they are circumspect in managing our economy after their post-Covid-19 experiences. They are bold to refuse influences and threats to do things that would plunge the economy into bad shape. I declare that their decisions and policies are always for the growth and development of our economy. Praise be to Your Holy Name. Father. Amen.

Further Reading: 1 Corinthians 10: 24

144. DECLARE GOD'S BLESSINGS ON YOUR BUSINESS OR JOB

Bible Passage

"May he grant you your heart's desire and fulfill all your plans" Psalm 20: 4.

In the Name of Jesus Christ, I pronounce God's blessings on my job, business and other means. I prophecy increased favor and grace from men and women of goodwill. The Name of the Lord Jesus Christ is named on my businesses. I make progress by the Spirit of God. All that I lay my hands on turns out to be a huge success. I receive calls and messages from genuine people for good businesses. The blessing of God that makes you rich without sorrows is upon my job and business in Jesus' Name. Amen.

Further Reading: Proverbs 16: 3.

145. PRAY FOR DESTINY HELPERS

Bible Passage

"The Lord is my strength and my strong helper, He has become my salvation: He is my God and I will give Him praise; my father's God and I will give Him glory" Exodus 15: 2.

I will look up to You, Lord God because my help comes from You. I declare that You are my strength and strong helper. I thank You, Lord, for the men, women, resources and circumstances you have divinely arranged and placed on my path to help me achieve things in my destiny. I pray that at every point, I will recognize and make full-proof of them to Your praise and glory in Jesus' Name. Amen.

Further Reading: Joshua 1: 1.

146. PRAY FOR OPPORTUNITIES TO EXPAND YOUR BUSINESS: DECLARE THAT YOU WILL SEE THE OPPORTUNITIES OTHERS DO NOT SEE

Bible Passage

"And God is able to make all grace abound to you, so that having all sufficiency in all things at all times, you may abound in every good work" 2 Corinthians 9: 8.

In the Name of Jesus Christ, I pray that by the Spirit of God, I will see opportunities for progress where others do not see. Like Isaac, who dug wells and found water where others did not, I see great chances to move my business forward and make progress. I declare that every move I make to expand my businesses succeeds. Every investment I make yields great profits by the Spirit of God. I have the yeast to grow and expand, and it is seen in my job and businesses. Praise God!

Further Reading: James 1: 17

147. PRAY FOR GOD'S SPECIAL FAVORS

Bible Passage

"For You, O Lord, will bless the righteous; with favor You will surround him as with a shield" Psalm 5: 12.

I thank You, dear Father, in Jesus' Name for blessing me with favor on every side. Lord, because of Your favor upon my life, good comes to me from far and near. Men are falling upon themselves to do me good. I receive financial favor from the folks I least expect money from. All that I lay my hands on are blessed because God's favor is upon my life. Men call me blessed because I am the favored of the Lord. Praise God forevermore.

Further Reading: Numbers 6: 25 – 26.

148. DECLARE THAT THE PRINCE OF THIS WORLD COMES BUT HE HAS NOTHING IN YOU AND YOUR BUSINESS OR JOB

Bible Passage

"I will no longer talk much with you, for the ruler of this world is coming, and he has nothing in Me" John 14: 30.

In the Name of the Lord Jesus Christ, I declare that the prince of this world system comes, but he has nothing in me or my businesses or job. The spoiler, devourer that wastes people's businesses comes, but he cannot spoil my businesses in Jesus' Name. I pay my tithes as and when they are due; thus, the devourer is restrained from wasting what belongs to me. My job or businesses are protected from inflation, depression or economic meltdowns. While others are going down, I and my businesses or job are lifted by the power of the Holy Spirit. Amen.

Further Reading: John 12: 31

149. PRAY FOR PRODUCTIVITY

Bible passage:

But my horn shall be exalted like a wild ox; I have been anointed with fresh oil...I shall flourish like a palm tree. I shall grow like a cedar in Lebanon. Those who are planted in the house of the Lord shall flourish in the courts of our God. They shall still bear fruit in old age; they shall be fresh and flourishing, to declare that the Lord is upright; He is my rock and there is no unrighteousness in Him. Psalm 92: 10-15

Your word said those that trust in the Lord are like trees planted beside the river; they will bring forth their fruits in their season. I renounce the life of dryness, emptiness, and death. I will flourish as a fresh fountain and blossom as the flowers of the river. Goodness and mercy will follow me all the days of my life. My hands are blessed, my steps are guided, my efforts are fruitful, and my commitments will birth enduring success. I will be a testimony of God's faithfulness, an expression of His grace, and a reference of His love. I decree life into my home, marriage, business, and career. I choose to live a full and productive life in Jesus' Name.

Further reading: *Jeremiah 29: 11-13 Colossians 3: 23, Proverbs 14: 23.*

150. PRAY TO RE-ASSIGNING ANGELS

Bible Passage

"Are not all angels ministering spirits sent to serve those who will inherit salvation?" Hebrews 1: 14.

In the Name of the Lord Jesus Christ, I dispatch angels to stir men and women to favor me. I command them to seek favorable business opportunities for me. I declare that from all over the world cause money and divine favor to locate me. God has given you charge over me so that I do not dash my foot against any stone. I command you to watch over me during the day and at night. Protect me and all that is mine from the attacks of the enemy. Halleluiah!

Further Reading: Psalm 91: 11.

Chapter 7: PRAYER FOR CHRISTIAN LIVING

The life you live among Christians and non-Christians speaks volumes of your profession as a Christian. Your life must show what you preach with your mouth. In other words, the Word of God must be seen to be working in your life. You cannot preach to others to love, when you do not love others. There is a purpose for your life, God's purpose. This purpose must reflect in your life and ministry as a Christian as an example to others around you. Remember what the Word of God says, 'Let your light so shine before men that they may see your good works and glorify your Father in heaven (Matthew 5: 16). Whatever you do, say or imply with your actions must reflect the personality of Christ-like life in you.

As you devote yourself to praying the prayers in this category, the Spirit of God will inspire God's wisdom in your heart to live the God-life in this world. You will live the Christian life by the power of the Holy Spirit to bring glory to God. Your life will spell the will of God. Your actions will be exemplary; people will see you and tell you that truly, you are a Christian. You will be able to fulfill God's desire for your life as you diligently pray these prayers by the Spirit. Your life can only be defined as divine or supernatural because men will not be able to explain you or your life.

151. PRAY FOR A PURPOSE-DRIVEN LIFE

Bible Passage

Many are the plans in a person's heart, but it is the Lord's purpose that prevails Proverbs 19: 21

I refuse to live my life according to my wisdom and understanding. You are the omniscient God, and you know the end even from the beginning. I come trusting and believing that you will help and guide me through the labyrinths of life. I cannot do it all alone. Grant me a courageous heart that cannot be intimidated or oppressed by the challenges of life. Help me to be confident in your love and unwavering faithfulness that I may unlock the secrets of an enduring financial, emotional, spiritual, and psychological breakthrough. Amen.

Further Reading: Exodus 9: 16, Job 42: 2.

152. PRAY TO DISCOVER CHRIST'S PURPOSE IN YOU

Bible Passage

"For we are His workmanship, created in Christ Jesus for good works, which God prepared beforehand, that we should walk in them" Ephesians 2: 10.

I am God's workmanship created in Christ Jesus. God has His preordained plans for my life; I am created to fulfill Christ's purpose for my life. I pray that I will discover every aspect of that purpose and fulfill it to the glory of God. I refuse to be distracted by the cares of this world or the devil. I am focused, and by the help of the Holy Spirit, I fulfill all that God has planned for me to achieve in this lifetime in Jesus' Name. Amen.

Further Reading: Jeremiah 29: 11.

153. PRAY FOR INSPIRATION

Bible Passage

"Trust in the LORD with all your heart, and do not lean on your own understanding. In all your ways acknowledge him, and he will make straight your paths" Proverbs 3: 5 – 6.

Blessed Father, I thank You for Your Spirit that is at work in me. He is my inspiration any time, any day. I declare that I will never be dry or short of ideas. The Extraordinary Strategist – the Holy Spirit in me, fills me with inspiration. I declare that I am always excited, and like David, I am excited about the things of God. I am inspired by new ideas and innovations about my job, business, home, marriage, relationships and life, in general, in Jesus' Name. Amen.

Further Reading: Joshua 1: 9.

154. PRAY FOR A NEW MOVE OF GOD

Bible Passage

"For it is God who is at work in you, both to will and to work for His good pleasure" Philippians 2: 13.

Blessed Father, I thank You because You are the One at work in me both to will and to do of Your good pleasure. I celebrate Your out-working in my life, a new move of God. I am inspired to sponsor Your work with the resourses You have blessed me with. I am inspired to win souls and encourage the spread of the Gospel all over the world. I declare that I am an end-time army of God, committed to seeing souls keep pouring into the Kingdom of God. Halleluiah!

Further Reading: John 13: 7.

155. PRAY FOR DIVINE UPLIFTMENT

Bible Passage

"I will be your God throughout your lifetime— until your hair is white with age. I made you, and I will care for you. I will carry you along and save you" Isaiah 46: 4.

Father, I am so overwhelmed with the assurance that You will remain my God throughout my lifetime. You assured me that You would take care of me, carry me along and save me. Blessed be Your Holy Name, Father. I thank You for divinely uplifting me in every facet of my life. Lord, I am grateful for Your blessings, love and peace. I declare that I am lifted; there is no shame for me. I am doing well in my business, ministry, marriage, finances, job, academics and relationship by the power of the Holy Spirit and in the Name of Jesus Christ. Amen.

Further Reading: Exodus 15: 2.

156. DECLARE THAT YOU ARE LIVING AN EXEMPLARY CHRISTIAN LIFE

Bible Passage

"In the same way, let your light shine before others, so that they may see your good works and give glory to your Father who is in heaven" Matthew 5: 16.

I declare by the power of the Holy Spirit that I am living a life worthy of emulation. I am living as a shining example to all those around me. I am an example of a good Christian in my world. My words, actions, views and dispositions show the world around me that I am Christ-like, and because of that, men are attracted to serve God. My way of life brings souls to the Kingdom of God. Halleluiah!!

Further Reading: 1 Peter 2: 21.

157. PRAY FOR THE RIGHT ATTITUDE

Bible Passage

"Finally, brothers, whatever is true, whatever is honorable, whatever is just, whatever is pure, whatever is lovely, whatever is commendable, if there is any excellence, if there is anything worthy of praise, think about these things" Philippians 4: 8 – 9.

Father, I thank You for teaching by Your Word the importance of having the right attitude. I declare that I am always conscious of my attitude towards others and the things of God. Your Word has taught me to dwell on thoughts that are true, honorable, just, pure, lovely, commendable, and excellent and praiseworthy. As I dwell on these things, I pray that they will produce wholesome words and actions through me in Jesus' Name. Amen.

Further Reading: Ephesians 4: 31 – 32.

158. PRAY FOR GOD'S GUIDANCE

Bible Passage

"The Lord is my shepherd; I shall not want. He makes me to lie down in green pastures: he leads me beside the still waters. He restores my soul: he leads me in the paths of righteousness for his name's sake" Psalm 23: 1 – 3.

Most Holy Father, I thank You for giving me Your Word and the Holy Spirit to guide. Your Word is a lamp to my feet and light to my path. I have no fear that I will fall because Your Word illuminates my paths. In all that I do, Your Holy Spirit is always with me to give me guidance. My ears are inclined to always listen and hear Your guidance in the mighty Name of the Lord Jesus Christ. Amen.

Further Reading: Isaiah 30: 21.

159. PRAYER OF CONTENTMENT

Bible Passage

"But godliness with contentment is great gain" 1 Timothy 6: 6.

Lord, I thank You for granting me the spirit of contentment. Your Word says that godliness with contentment is great gain. I thank You because I am contented with such things that You have blessed me with. The Lord Jesus Christ is my sufficiency; all that I need to live the good life, I have in abundance. I am blessed to be a blessing; God, channel of uplifting others. I thank You for this grace, precious Father in Jesus' Name. Amen.

Further Reading: Philippians 4: 11.

160. PRAY FOR SPIRITUAL PERFECTION

Bible Passage

"And let steadfastness have its full effect, that you may be perfect and complete, lacking in nothing" James 1: 4.

Father God, I thank You because I am complete in You. My perfection is of You. I do not lack anything because Christ is my sufficiency. I am perfect because I am the righteousness of God in Christ Jesus. Sin has no dominance in my spirit or mind. My thoughts and words are pure; they are seasoned with grace through and through. My mind is dominated by God's Word, and it reflects in all that I do or say in Jesus' Name. Amen.

Further Reading: Ephesians 4: 13.

161. PRAY TO IGNITE THE FIRE IN YOU

Bible Passage

"For this reason I remind you to fan into flame the gift of God, which is in you through the laying on of my hands" 2 Timothy 1: 6.

Heavenly Father, I declare that I am afire for You. I refuse to be cold or lukewarm but hot for the Lord. No matter the circumstances, I am on fire for the work of the ministry. I am an ardent soul winner, fervent in spirit, serving the Lord. I seek the advancement of the Kingdom with all that God has blessed me with. I am making full proof of my calling in the precious Name of Jesus Christ. Amen.

Further Reading: 1 Timothy 4: 14.

162. PRAY FOR CHANGE

Bible Passage

"For everything there is a season, and a time for every matter under heaven" Ecclesiastics 3: 1.

Precious Father, I thank You for the dynamic ability of Your Word to cause the desired change I need in my life through the Holy Spirit. As I meditate on Your Word day and night, I declare that there is a metamorphosis in every area of my life. There is a transformation in my health, finances, relationships, marriage, business and job; my life conforming to Your Word concerning me in the mighty Name of the Lord Jesus Christ.

Further Reading: Jeremiah 29: 11.

163. PRAYER TO BE RE-ENERGIZED FOR THE WORK

Bible Passage

"You shall remember the Lord your God, for it is he who gives you power to get wealth, that he may confirm his covenant that he swore to your fathers, as it is this day" Deuteronomy 8: 18.

I thank You, dear Father, for re-energizing me for the work of the ministry through the Holy Spirit. I'm not slothful in the Lord's business; rather, I am stirred for the work of the ministry. I recognize the harvest is plenteous, and I am re-energized as a laborer for the harvest of souls into the Kingdom of God. My finances, skills, time, abilities and life are for the work of the ministry. This is my purpose, what I was born to do. I thank You, Father, in Jesus' Name. Amen.

Further Reading: Philippians 4: 13.

164. DECLARE THAT YOU HAVE THE MIND OF CHRIST, AND IT SHOWS IN YOUR DISPOSITION

Bible Passage

"Let this mind be in you, which was also in Christ Jesus" Philippians 2: 5.

In the Name of the Lord Jesus Christ, I declare that I have the mind of Christ. My mind is dominated by the Word of God and His liquid love. I deal with people based on the Word of God in my heart. I love and value all people without any atom of hate or dislike for anyone. With humility, I am willing and ready to serve others. I go the extra mile for others to the glory of God and the blessing of humanity. I thank You, dear Father. Amen.

Further Reading: 2 Corinthians 4: 6.

165. PRAY FOR EXCELLENCE

Bible Passage

"*Now for this very reason also, applying all diligence, in your faith supply moral excellence, and in your moral excellence, knowledge*" 2 Peter 1: 5

Father, I thank You for the Spirit of excellence in me. I do things that turn out excellently. My thoughts, words, actions and perceptions are products of the Spirit of excellence in me. The things I do are marked with excellence; they produce praise and honor to God almighty. I declare that men and women from far and near are drawn to me because of the excellence I produce from my spirit in Jesus' Name. Amen.

Further Reading: 1 Corinthians 12: 31

166. PRAY THAT THE BOND OF UNITY AMONG CHRISTIANS WILL BECOME STRONGER

Bible Passage

"*All the believers were one in heart and mind. No one claimed that any of their possessions was their own, but they shared everything they had*" Acts 4: 32.

Father God, I thank You for the bond of unity and love we have amongst us as Christians. I pray that this bond grows stronger, and Christians all over the world see themselves as one big family of God. I pray, Lord, that Your Spirit will bind all Christians and cause us to see beyond our denominations. I declare that we would rather focus on the truth that binds us instead of things that tear us apart in Jesus' Name. Amen.

Further Reading: Galatians 3: 28.

167. PRAY FOR MEN OF GOODWILL

Bible Passage

"Glory to God in the highest heaven, and on earth peace to those on whom his favor rests" Luke 2: 14.

Father God, I thank You especially for all men and women of goodwill; yes, for the brethren scattered all over the world who seek my good and wish me well. I pray that You might Hand rest upon them. I declare that they are blessed with Your divine grace, wisdom and presence. I pray that nothing shall be said to be too good for them. Whatever they do, they shall prosper with unusual testimonies in Jesus' Name. Amen.

Further Reading: Philippians 2: 13.

168. DECLARE THAT YOU ALWAYS WALK IN GOD'S LOVE

Bible Passage

"And now these three remain: faith, hope and love. But the greatest of these is love" 1 Corinthians 13: 13.

Lord God, by the authority I have in the Name of the Lord Jesus Christ, I declare that always, I walk in Your love. I see others with the eyes of love. Lord, Your love is what motivates me to win souls and help those in need. Your love has been shed abroad in my heart, and it flows through me to touch others. Through me, my world is experiencing God's liquid love that saves, blesses, helps and uplifts those that receive it. Blessed be God!

Further Reading: 1 John 4: 9 – 10.

169. PRAYER FOR CONTINUOUS SAFETY

Bible Passage

"Whoever dwells in the shelter of the Most High will rest in the shadow of the Almighty. I will say of the Lord, "He is my refuge and my fortress, my God, in whom I trust" Psalm 91: 1 – 2.

Blessed Father, in the Name of the Lord Jesus, I am thankful because You are my dwelling place, and under Your shadow, I will always find safety. I trust in You because You are my shelter, refuge and my fortress. Lord, my safety is guaranteed in You. You are my Rock, and there is no fear in my heart concerning my safety. I thank You, Lord, for always having my back in my going out and coming in. My life and all that is mine are secured and fortified in You. Blessed be Your Name forevermore.

Further Reading: 2 Thessalonians 3: 3.

170. PRAY THAT THE LOVE OF GOD THAT IS SHED ABROAD IN YOUR HEART FLOWS AS LIQUID LOVE TO OTHERS AROUND YOU

Bible Passage

"Now hope does not disappoint, because the love of God has been poured out in our hearts by the Holy Spirit who was given to us" Romans 5: 5.

Father God, I pray especially for so many who are alien to Your liquid love, those who have been beaten and wounded by the circumstances of life or their own mistakes. Some the devil and their frail consciences have lied to them that You cannot accept them again. I pray that through me, many will yet experience Your love again. I declare that they will accept Your love and receive salvation for their souls in Jesus' Name. Amen.

Further Reading: Matthew 5: 9.

171. PRAY THAT YOU ARE ABLE TO LIVE IN PEACE WITH YOUR NEIGHBORS AND COLLEAGUES

Bible Passage

"*If possible, so far as it depends on you, live peaceably with all*" Romans 12: 18.

Father, in the Name of the Lord Jesus Christ, I pray that I am always able to live in peace with others. Be the person my neighbor, friend, colleague or whoever, I can live and coexist with him or her in peace as the Word of God enjoins. I pray that every difficult person that comes my way is overwhelmed with the love of God I will show him or her. By the power of the Holy Spirit at work in me, no one would be able to resist my love. Amen.

Further Reading: Mark 9: 50.

172. PRAY TO UPHOLD THE TRUTH AT ALL TIMES

Bible Passage

"I have no greater joy than to hear that my children are walking in the truth" 3 John 1: 4.

I thank You, dear Father, for Your grace that is at work in me. I declare that in the Name of the Lord Jesus and the help of the Holy Spirit, I will always uphold the truth of the Gospel at all times. No matter the opposition, I will stand my ground on the truth. Your Word says, 'I will know the truth, and it will make me free.' Therefore, I declare that I am for the truth, and I stand for it always in the Name of Jesus Christ. Amen.

Further Reading: Psalm 15: 2 – 3.

173. DECLARE THAT THERE IS NOBODY YOU CANNOT LOVE

Bible Passage

"A new command I give you: Love one another. As I have loved you, so you must love one another" John 13: 34.

In the Name of the Lord Jesus Christ, I declare that there is nobody I cannot love. I am exactly like the Lord Jesus Christ, and I love the same way He loves. With the love of God I have in my heart and the Word of God in my spirit, loving others is very easy for me. I am born of God, who is love personified. Therefore, I can love anyone regardless of their shortcomings. I thank You, Father, for this rare privilege. Amen.

Further Reading: Matthew 5: 44.

174. PRAYER OF PRAISE AND WORSHIP

Bible Passage

"All the earth will worship You, and will sing praises to You; they will sing praises to Your Name" Psalm 66: 4.

Father, I praise and worship You for Your awesome greatness. You are the maker of all things; You preexisted the beginning. Eternity is within Your space, and there is none like You. Your love for me is unfathomable; it is deeper than the ocean depth and higher than the high heavens. Lord God, I love You with the whole of my heart, the whole of my existence. You are the King of kings and the Lord of Lords. You are the author and giver of life. Lord, I am grateful to You for everything in Jesus' Name. Amen.

Further Reading: Psalm 86: 12.

175. DECLARE THAT YOU ARE LIVING ACCORDING TO THE WORD OF GOD

Bible Passage

"But He answered and said, "It is written, "Man shall not live by bread alone, but by every word that proceeds from the mouth of God" Matthew 4: 4.

In the Name of the Lord Jesus, I declare that I am a Christian, and I live according to the Word of God. The Word of God is my source and life, and I can only live accordingly. Praise God! I declare that all that I do or say, the Word of God emanates from me. I am not just a hearer of the Word of God; I am a doer, a Word practitioner. I reflect God everywhere I go; I am the Word of God to my world. Blessed be God! Halleluiah!

Further Reading: 1 Peter 2: 2.

176. DECLARE THAT YOU ARE DEAD TO SIN AND ALIVE TO RIGHTEOUSNESS

Bible Passage

"Who his own self bare our sins in his own body on the tree that we, <u>being dead to sins, should live unto righteousness</u>: by whose stripes ye were healed" 1 Peter 2: 24.

In the Name of the Lord Jesus Christ, I declare that I am dead to sin and alive to righteousness. I am holy, sanctified and righteous. The Lord Jesus Christ has been made my righteousness, wisdom and sanctification. Sin does not have any power over me. I live to please the God of my salvation, the God that called me out of darkness and translated me into the Kingdom of His dear Son Jesus Christ. I do not live to please my flesh or the rudiments of this world but God. Glory to You, blessed Father, Amen.

Further Reading: Romans 6: 11.

177. PRAY YOU WILL NOT LIVE A LIFE OF COMPLAINTS AND WORTHLESS ARGUMENTS

Bible Passage

"Do everything without complaining or arguing, so that you may become blameless and pure, children of God without fault in a crooked and depraved generation, in which you shine like stars in the universe" Philippians 2: 14 – 15.

Father God, I thank You for the glorious life You have granted me to live. I please You and You alone with my life. In the Name of the Lord Jesus Christ, I do not live a life of complaints and arguments, but I live a blameless life as a child of God without faults. I live an exciting life; I please God with a sanctified heart that is full of love in Jesus' Name. Amen.

Further Reading: 1 Corinthians 10: 10.

178. PRAY AND DECLARE THAT YOUR LIFE WILL MINISTER AND ATTRACT SINNERS TO CHRIST

Bible Passage

"You are our epistle written in our hearts, known and read by all men" 2 Corinthians 3: 2.

Father, I thank You because my life and the way I live minister and attract sinners to give their lives to You. Your Word says I am the light of the world. This is my experience, Lord. I shine forth Your life, and sinners cannot but troop to receive Christ as their Lord and Savior. Men see the good works that I do, and they flood in to accept Jesus into their hearts to the glory of God. I thank You, Father, in Jesus' Name. Amen.

Further Reading: Romans 1: 8.

179. PRAY THAT YOU FUNCTION IN GRACE: YOU WILL NOT DO ANYTHING OUT OF SELFISH AMBITION

Bible Passage

"Do nothing out of selfish ambition or vain conceit, but in humility consider others better than yourselves" Philippians 2: 3.

Father, I declare that by the power of the Holy Spirit, enjoy more grace to do and achieve more exploits in life. I refuse to do anything out of selfish ambitions. I have more grace for ministry, business, family, relationships and all that I want to achieve. In the Name of the Lord Jesus Christ, I have the men, materials, finances and circumstances to help me achieve my goals. I do not struggle to get or achieve anything; I function by grace. Amen.

Further Reading: Romans 12: 10.

180. PRAY FOR MORE OPPORTUNITIES TO WIN SOULS FOR THE LORD

Bible Passage

"*Knowing therefore the terror of the Lord, we persuade men; but we are made manifest unto God; and I trust also are made manifest in your consciences*" 2 Corinthians 5: 11.

Praise God! Father, I thank You for the many opportunities You have granted me to win souls. I declare that I do not take these opportunities lightly I recognize the worth of a soul. You sent the Lord Jesus to die for the souls of men. I know that if it were just one soul, the Lord would still have died for it. I pray that any soul I reach out to gladly receive salvation to be saved. I am instrumental to the depopulation of the kingdom of darkness in Jesus' Name. Amen.

Further Reading: 1 Corinthians 16: 6.

181. DECLARE THAT IT IS NOT DIFFICULT FOR YOU TO HELP OTHERS

Bible Passage

"*Do not neglect to do good and to share what you have, for such sacrifices are pleasing to God*" Hebrews 13: 16.

I thank You, Precious Father, for the grace to help people that I have received from You. I declare that it is not difficult for me to help others. I deal with people based on the love of God that flows from my heart. No matter who the person is, as long as it is within my ability to help the person, I do so with gladness. I declare that I am the Lord's outstretched hand to help folks out of their predicaments in Jesus' Name. Amen.

Further Reading: Philippians 2: 4.

182. DECLARE THAT YOU ARE GOD'S WORKMANSHIP CREATED IN CHRIST JESUS UNTO GOOD WORKS

Bible Passage

"For we are His workmanship, created in Christ Jesus for good works, which God prepared beforehand that we should walk in them" Ephesians 2: 10.

Blessed Father, I thank You for the privilege of being Your instrument for good works. I am Your workmanship created in Christ Jesus unto good works, which You prepared for me to walk in them. I pray that at every level in life, I receive increased grace to manifest the excellent works of God to my world. My light is shining so brightly, and men are seeing my good works and giving glory to God the Father in Jesus' Name. Amen.

Further Reading: Matthew 5: 16.

183. PRAY FOR GRACE TO BE MORE HUMBLE

Bible Passage

"But he gives us more grace. That is why Scripture says: "God opposes the proud but shows favor to the humble" James 4: 6.

Lord God, I thank You for more grace to be humble, especially in the face of provocations. Your Word says You resist the proud but give more grace to the humble. I ask Lord for more of Your grace to deal with the issues of life. I rebuke every proud spirit. I am humble, submissive and calm in spirit. In whatever situation, I display humility the same way the Lord Jesus would have if He were faced with the same situation. I thank You, Father, for more grace in Jesus' Name. Amen.

Further Reading: 1 Peter 5: 5.

184. DECLARE THAT YOU ARE AN IMITATOR OF CHRIST: YOU PUT THE WORD OF GOD TO PRACTICE

Bible Passage

"For you have been called for this purpose, since Christ also suffered for you, leaving you an example for you to follow in His steps" 1 Peter 2: 21.

I am an imitator of Christ because I am born of God. In Christ, I live, move and have my being. I am Christ-like in all my dispositions. When men see me, they know without any inhibitions that I am a Christian because of my way of life. My words are seasoned with grace. My words bring life to those that hear me or the folks I address. Whoever I pray for to receive healing gets healed instantly. By the Spirit of God, I pull men and women to receive Christ as their Lord and Savior. Praise God!

Further Reading: 1 Corinthians 11: 1.

185. DECLARE THAT YOU ARE DILIGENT IN ALL THINGS

Bible Passage:

"*The soul of the sluggard craves and gets nothing, while the soul of the diligent is richly supplied*" Proverbs 13: 4.

Heavenly Father, You said in 1 Corinthians 14: 40 that we should do everything decently and in order. I thank You for instilling in me an excellent spirit. I declare that I am diligent in all that I do. All that I set my hands to do turn out excellently because I do them diligently. I do the right thing, the first time, the right way and for the right reasons by the Spirit of God at work in me. I am not scattered but diligent and decent in Jesus' Name. Amen.

Further Reading: Proverbs 12: 24.

186. DECLARE THAT YOUR AFFECTION IS TOWARDS GOD AND NOT ON THINGS OF THIS WORLD

Bible Passage

"For this reason I remind you to kindle afresh the gift of God which is in you through the laying on of my hands" 2 Timothy 1: 6.

Father, I thank You for creating in me the right will and passion to seek after You. I declare that my affections, love and zeal are towards You only. My desire is to do Your will, to fulfill Your Word and bring You honor and praise. I declare that my life, skills, and resources are for Your worship and praise. I live to please You, my heavenly Father, I thank You for this awesome honor and privilege in Jesus' Name. Amen.

Further Reading: Revelation 3: 19.

187. PRAY THAT BY THE SPIRIT OF GOD, YOU WILL ONLY KEEP THE RIGHT COMPANIES

Bible Passage

"Do not be deceived: "Bad company corrupts good character" 1 Corinthians 15: 33.

Lord God, I thank You for giving me the Holy Spirit. I pray that by Your Spirit, I am able to live a true Christian life. I pray that Your Spirit that is at work in me will always help me make the right friends and companies. Your Word says bad company corrupts good character. I declare that my excellent character is intact. No wrong friends or colleagues can distract me or corrupt my good character in Jesus' Name. Amen.

Further Reading: 1 Corinthians 6: 9; Proverbs 22: 25.

188. PRAYER FOR THE SALVATION OF SOULS

Bible Passage

"Neither is there salvation in any other: for there is none other name under heaven given among men, whereby we must be saved" Acts 4: 12.

Father God, In the Name of the Lord Jesus Christ, I pray for the salvation of souls in these perilous times. So many are afraid, suspicious, and their heart is failing them. So many do not know what to do and thus have become susceptible to the deception of the enemy. I pray that the light of the glorious Gospel of Christ shines in their hearts. I pray that they will gladly receive salvation and be saved. I thank You, Lord. Amen.

Further Reading: Acts 16: 30 – 31.

189. PRAY FOR COMFORT

Bible Passage

"For whatever things were written before were written for our learning, that we through the patience and comfort of the Scriptures might have hope" Romans 15: 4.

Father, I thank You for sending us the Holy Spirit as our comforter. He is our dependable companion any time, any day. Lord, I pray for as many who are in one dilemma or another that they will find comfort in Your Word and Spirit You have given us. I pray that they will be guided to seek comfort in the Holy Spirit instead of running to the wrong sources being pushed to them by the world. I thank You, Lord in Jesus' Name. Amen.

Further Reading: Matthew 11: 28.

190. PRAY FOR CONVERSION OF SINNERS

Bible Passage

"For the Lord your God is gracious and compassionate. He will not turn his face from you if you return to him" 2 Chronicles 30: 9b.

Gracious Father, I thank You for sending the Lord Jesus Christ to die for our sins and to bring us into oneness with You. Father, I pray for sinners all around the world, especially for the ones in my world of contact. I pray that the light of the glorious Gospel of Christ shines on them. I pray that with a great rush, they accept the Lord Jesus as their Lord and Savior. Today is their day of salvation. I declare that everything inhibiting them is removed, and gladly, they are saved in the mighty Name of Jesus Christ. Amen.

Further Reading: 2 Peter 3: 9.

191. PRAY FOR SUCCESS IN ALL YOUR ENDEAVOURS

Bible Passage

"*Delight yourself in the* L*ord*, *and he will give you the desires of your heart*" Psalm 37: 4

In the mighty Name of the Lord Jesus Christ, I declare that I am a huge success. I succeed in all that I lay my hands to do; all my endeavors in life turn out to be a great success. The Lord has blessed me with all that pertains to life and godliness – yes, the yeast to rise is in me. I make progress because the oil of success is upon my head. I am highly favored, and I can only succeed. Glory to God!

Further Reading: Proverb 16: 3.

Chapter 8: PRAYER FOR THE LOVE OF GOD

As a Christian, I realize that the love of God has been shed abroad in your heart by the Holy Spirit that lives in your heart. There is nobody you cannot love. The love of God exists in your heart in liquid form. It flows unhindered from you to others, helping them experience God in a fashion they never knew. No matter how wicked the fellow is, you can love him and use the love of God to bring him to the fold of Christ. In other words, as you show the world around the unfailing love of God, many will be brought in to receive God's salvation for their souls.

Also, God has shown us how to love others by giving us Jesus Christ to die for our sins. We can love others sacrificially the same way God has shown us to love others around us. He has not only commanded us to love, but He gave us the Holy Spirit to teach and help us love others. Now, by the Spirit of God, you can extend God's love to your world and have lives touched and changed to the glory of God.

The Spirit of God has arranged these prayers to cause the demonstration of love rather than mere words. It is one thing to say you love someone and another to show the person God's love. As you pray, you will find yourself acting out God's love to others effortlessly. People will look at you and testify that you are indeed a child of God.

192. PRAY THAT THE LOVE OF GOD WILL SHIELD YOU FROM ALL HARMS

Bible Passage

"But let all who take refuge in You rejoice; let them sing joyful praises forever. Spread Your protection over them, that all who love Your name may be filled with joy. For You bless the godly, O LORD; You surround them with Your shield of love" Psalm 5:11 – 12.

Father God, I thank You for the immeasurable love that You have for me. In my going out and coming in, Your love keeps me safe from all harms. When I travel, I rely on Your love for my safety. You protect me from all the snares of the enemy because of Your unfailing love. You not only spread Your love to me but also to my family. Lord, Your compassion over us is overwhelming, and I love You more and more in Jesus' Name. Amen.

Further Reading: Psalm 32: 7.

193. DECLARE THAT NOTHING CAN REMOVE YOU FROM THE LOVE OF GOD

Bible Passage

"Who shall separate us from the love of Christ? Shall trouble or hardship or persecution or famine or nakedness or danger or sword?" Romans 8: 35.

Blessed Father, I thank You because, by the Holy Spirit, I am sustained by Your love. I declare that no force or circumstances on earth, in the heavens, or under the earth shall be able to separate me from Your love. No matter how fierce the trial or persecution, nothing shall be able to detach me from Your love.

In the Name of the Lord Jesus Christ, I am forever connected to You, Father, bounded to You through Your precious love. Praise God forevermore. Halleluiah! Amen.

Further Reading: Romans 8: 37.

194. DECLARE THAT THE LOVE OF GOD CAST OUT ALL FEARS FROM YOUR HEART

Bible Passage

"Such love has no fear, because perfect love expels all fear. If we are afraid, it is for fear of punishment, and this shows that we have not fully experienced His perfect love" 1 John 4: 18.

Precious Father, I thank You because You have not given me the spirit of fear but the Spirit of love, boldness and sound mind. I declare that Your love in me dispels all fear from my heart. In the Name of the Lord Jesus Christ, my heart is full of love. Therefore, by the power of the Holy Spirit at work in me, I declare with all boldness that my system does not accommodate fear or doubts. The peace that comes from the love of God garrisons my heart always in Jesus' Name. Amen.

Further Reading: Romans 8: 15.

195. PRAY THAT YOU WILL ALWAYS EXHIBIT THE CHARACTERISTICS OF LOVE

Bible Passage

"Love is patient and kind. Love is not jealous or boastful or proud or rude. It does not demand its own way. It is not irritable, and it keeps no record of being wronged. It does not rejoice about injustice but rejoices whenever the truth wins out. Love never gives up, never loses faith, is always hopeful, and endures through every circumstance" 1 Corinthians 13: 4 – 7.

Dear Lord, I praise You with my life because words are not enough. You have filled my heart and life with Your love, and now and forever, I will always praise You. Lord, I pray that by Your Spirit that is in my heart, I will continually exhibit the characteristics of Your love. I declare that I am patient, kind, not rude or proud; I do not keep records of wrong or being irritable; I do not rejoice over injustice but in truth. I do not give up or lose faith in Jesus' Name. Amen.

Further Reading: Proverbs 10: 12.

196. PRAY TO PERFECTLY UNDERSTAND GOD'S LOVE

Bible Passage

"*And may you have the power to understand, as all God's people should, how wide, how long, how high, and how deep His love is. May you experience the love of Christ, though it is too great to understand fully. Then you will be made complete with all the fullness of life and power that comes from God*" Ephesians 3: 18 – 19.

Lord God, so many are in a serious dilemma today because they fail to understand Your love for them. I pray that more and more, I have the power to understand the height and depth of Your love and comprehend all its dimensions. I thank You, Father, because daily, I will experience Your love so that I can be made perfect in it. A better understanding of Your love inspires me to love everyone I come in contact with in Jesus' Name. Amen.

Further Reading: Job 11: 7 – 8.

197. THANK GOD BECAUSE HE KEEPS YOU WITH HIS LOVE

Bible Passage

"Your unfailing love, O LORD, is as vast as the heavens; your faithfulness reaches beyond the clouds. Your righteousness is like the mighty mountains, Your justice like the ocean depths. You care for people and animals alike, O LORD. How precious is Your unfailing love, O God! All humanity finds shelter in the shadow of Your wings" Psalm 36: 5 – 7.

I thank You, Lord, for keeping me in Your love-fold. With Your unfailing love, You showered me with so many blessings, privileges and opportunities. Through Your love, I have met with so many people that You have used to bless me. I have also become a channel of Your blessings to so many. Lord, in all, You have kept and sustained me in and with Your love through the power of the Holy Spirit. Father, I bless Your Holy Name forever in the Name of the Lord Jesus Christ. Amen.

Further Reading: Psalm 89: 2.

198. THANK GOD FOR LOVING YOU PERSONALLY

Bible Passage

"See how very much our Father loves us, for He calls us His children, and that is what we are! But the people who belong to this world don't recognize that we are God's children because they don't know Him" 1 John 3: 1.

Father, I thank You for loving me personally. I know, Father, if I were the only one on planet earth, You still would have loved me and sent the Lord Jesus Christ to die to save me. Lord, this knowledge means so much to me. With many instances, You have proven Your sweet and sincere love to me. You kept me in perfect health by Your love. I have experienced countless miracles that I can only trace to Your love for me. Blessed Father, from the bottom of my heart, I profusely thank You in Jesus' Name. Amen.

Further Reading: Luke 20: 36.

199. THANK GOD FOR ADOPTING YOU INTO HIS FAMILY BECAUSE OF HIS LOVE FOR YOU

Bible Passage

"God decided in advance to adopt us into His own family by bringing us to Himself through Jesus Christ. This is what He wanted to do, and it gave Him great pleasure" Ephesians 1: 5.

Father, You are the only wise God. I thank You for deciding to adopt me into Your own family before the foundations of the world. You brought me to Yourself through the Lord Jesus Christ, who did not mind the shame, and with love, died to save me. I am so grateful, Father, because the reason I am a born again Christian today is by Your special grace. You counted me worthy of being called Your son. Blessed be Your Name in Jesus' Name. Amen.

Further Reading: Luke 12: 32.

200. THANK GOD FOR HIS LOVE SACRIFICE FOR YOU

Bible Passage

"*For this is how God loved the world: He gave His one and only Son, so that everyone who believes in Him will not perish but have eternal life*" John 3: 16.

Father God, in the Name of the Lord Jesus Christ, I thank You for Your love sacrifice for me. Your Word says 'that You so loved the world that You gave Jesus to die for our sins.' Lord, I dare to personalize this sacrifice, and I am so grateful to You, Father, that I have accepted the Lord Jesus as my Savior, and now I have eternal life. I have the life and nature of God. I have the Holy Spirit in my heart. By the Lord Jesus, I have wisdom; I am holy and righteous. Praise be to God! Amen.

Further Reading: Genesis 22: 2.

201. THANK GOD FOR LOVING YOU EVEN WHEN YOU WERE UNDESERVING

Bible Passage

"But God is so rich in mercy, and He loved us so much, that even though we were dead because of our sins, He gave us life when He raised Christ from the dead. (It is only by God's grace that you have been saved!" Ephesians 2: 4 – 5.

Lord God, Your Word says, by Your mercy, You loved 'me,' even when I was dead in sin. You sent Jesus to die and to deliver me out of the domain of darkness; the clutches of the devil and sin, and translated me into the Kingdom of light; You own the Kingdom. Lord, even as I mature in Your Word, with love, You forgave my shortcomings; You kept me in Your love-fold family. I thank You so much, Father, in the Name of the Lord Jesus Christ. Amen.

Further Reading: Romans 5: 8.

202. DECLARE THAT THE LOVE OF GOD ENHANCES YOUR CHRISTIAN GROWTH

Bible Passage

"Either way, Christ's love controls us. Since we believe that Christ died for all, we also believe that we have all died to our old life. He died for everyone so that those who receive His new life will no longer live for themselves. Instead, they will live for Christ, who died and was raised for them" 2 Corinthians 5: 14 – 15.

In the Name of the Lord Jesus Christ, I declare that with the love of God in my heart, I will love God more and love God's people. His love will continually stir me to know more about God through His Word. I will do everything by God's Word. I will win souls, help others and be a blessing to my world through the love of God in my heart. My manifestation of God's love enhances my Christian growth by the power of the Holy Spirit. Hallelujah! Amen.

Further Reading: Jeremiah 31: 3.

203. THANK GOD FOR GIVING YOU THE HOLY SPIRIT TO HELP YOU EXPRESS HIS LOVE

Bible Passage

"And hope does not put us to shame, because God's love has been poured out into our hearts through the Holy Spirit, who has been given to us" Romans 5: 5.

Blessed Father, I thank You for graciously giving me the Holy Spirit. Today, I am able to express Your love with the help of the Holy Spirit. The Holy Spirit teaches me Your Word and shows me how to work it out in love. Now, there is no one I do not love because the Holy Spirit uses the Word to show me who they really are – God's love beings. Father, I praise Your Majesty for this awesomeness, the Name of the Lord Jesus Christ. Amen.

Further Reading: 1 John 3: 1.

204. PRAY FOR MORE GRACE TO ACCEPT THE LOVE CHASTENING OF THE LORD

Bible Passage

"For whom the LORD loves He chastens, And scourges every son whom He receives" Hebrews 12: 6.

Everlasting Father, I thank You for giving me more grace as I require in my Christian walk. Now, I pray for more grace to gladly accept Your love chastening. Your Word says, 'You chasten the one You love; You scourge the son You receive.' I declare that I will gladly receive Your chastening because I know it is for my good. It is meant to mature me, to prune me of dead works and bring me into Your perfect will for my life. I thank You Holy Father in Jesus' Name. Amen.

Further Reading: Proverbs 3: 11.

205. PRAY THAT THE LOVE OF GOD WILL SUSTAIN YOU IN DIFFICULT TIMES

Bible Passage

"I will be glad and rejoice in your unfailing love, for you have seen my troubles, and you care about the anguish of my soul" Psalm 31: 7.

Lord God, I thank You, in the Name of Jesus Christ, for the sustenance of Your unfailing love. I pray that in difficult times, Your love will sustain me in Your perfect will. I declare that nothing is able to sway me from the path You have marked out for me to walk in life. Your love guards my feet through any situation I have to go through in my faith walk. I am sustained by God's love in His will. Halleluiah! Praise God! Amen.

Further Reading: Psalm 118: 24.

206. DECLARE THAT THERE IS NO HOPELESS SITUATION FOR YOU BECAUSE OF THE LOVE OF GOD

Bible Passage

"Because of the LORD's great love we are not consumed, for his compassions never fail. They are new every morning; great is Your faithfulness!"

In the Name of the Lord Jesus Christ, I declare by the power of the Holy Spirit that there is no hopeless situation for me in life. I am a child of God – an heir of God and joint heir with Christ Jesus. Hence, I can never be disadvantaged; there is no hopeless situation for me. The love of the Father keeps me strong and on fire. I have the consciousness of a victor, a winner, because I walk in God's love always. Praise God forevermore. Amen.

Further Reading: Psalm 103: 10.

207. DECLARE THAT YOU DO EVERYTHING IN LOVE

Bible Passage

"*Do everything in love*" 1 Corinthians 16: 14.

Glorious Father, I thank You because in all that I do, I do them in love. There is no room for hate or resentment for anyone in my heart because it is full of love. My words are full of love. When I speak to people, I speak forth God's love to them. Yes, when men hear me, they hear God's love. I do my works with love; in all that I do, by the Spirit I demonstrate God's love in Jesus' Name. Amen.

Further Reading: Colossians 3: 14.

208. DECLARE THAT YOU CAN LOVE OTHERS THE SAME WAY GOD LOVES YOU

Bible Passage

"Hereby perceive we the love of God, because he laid down his life for us: and we ought to lay down our lives for the brethren" 1 John 3: 16.

I am God's love child. The Father has shown me how to love by sending the Lord Jesus to die for me personally. Now, the love of God has been shed abroad in my heart. I can love others selflessly the same way God loves me. I can go the extra mile for others. I refuse to equate people with their mistakes or shortcomings. I see them the way God sees them, with a love lens. Praise God! Halleluiah!

Further Reading: 1 John 4: 10.

209. PRAY THAT THE LOVE OF GOD CONSTRAINS YOU TO BE KINGDOM-MINDED

Bible Passage

"For the love of Christ compels us, because we judge thus: that if One died for all, then all died" 2 Corinthians 5: 14.

Father, I know that these are perilous times; the days are evil. Lord, I pray that no matter what, Your love constrains me to be about Your work, to be kingdom-minded. The love of God for sinners constrains me from reaching out to the unsaved with the Gospel, which is the power of God unto salvation. With the love of God in my heart, I will use my finances and other resources to sponsor the Gospel to the ends of the earth in Jesus' Name. Amen.

Further Reading: Acts 18: 5.

210. DECLARE THAT YOU ARE A LOVE BEING FROM GOD WHO IS LOVE

Bible Passage

"*Dear friends, let us love one another, for love comes from God. Everyone who loves has been born of God and knows God*" 1 John 4: 7.

I declare that I am an offspring of love. God is love, and I am by love begotten of a love God. Thus, I cannot love anyone I come in contact with. My breath, words, actions, thoughts, contemplations are all infused with love. I express love everywhere at anytime without any reservations. The Word of God in my heart helps express love as a love being in this cynical world. I thank You, dear Father, because You are more than a loving Father, You are love. Praise God! Amen.

Further Reading: 1 Corinthians 8: 3.

211. PRAY FOR THE LOVE OF GOD TO COVER THE HEARTS OF MEN

Bible Passage

"*His banner over me is love*" Song of Songs 2: 4.

Father, You are the Sovereign God. You are love personified. I pray, precious Father, that Your love overwhelms men's hearts in these last days. I declare that rather than men's hearts failing them because of the wickedness in the world today, their hearts are mantled with Your love. I pray that men will love their brothers and sisters again; they will do righteousness and prove the world wrong. I declare that God's love wins it at all times for me by the power of the Holy Spirit in Jesus' Name. Amen.

Further Reading: 1 Peter 4: 8.

Chapter 9: PRAYING FOR YOUR FAMILY

It is very important that you learn to stand in the gap for your family as a child of God. Do not assume someone else in your family is doing it. Even when you know that your dad or mum or someone else is always praying for your family, still stand out in the gap because prayers can never be too much. It is an honor, a rare privilege to be the one the Spirit of God can prompt to wake up in the night to pray for everyone else in your family.

In this section of prayers, you will have the opportunity to pray for the salvation of those who are not saved in your family, and they would receive the Lord Jesus Christ as Lord and Savior. You will have the chance to pray for their protection, health, unity, love, and so much more. As a result of your prayers, there will be so much prosperity in your family.

Death will be removed, and there will be so much joy, peace, blessing, grace, divine health, righteousness and grace. The Hand of God will be seen so strong in your family.

Ensure you pray fervently for your family and see visions of your prayers coming to pass in the lives of everyone in your family. God is keen on seeing your family whole, and that is why you are the one who came in contact with these prayers. So, with faith in your heart, pray and be expectant.

212. PRAY THAT YOUR FAMILY IS KEPT SAFE BY THE POWER OF GOD IN THESE LAST DAYS

Bible Passage

"But the Lord is faithful, and he will strengthen you and protect you from the evil one." 2 Thessalonians 3: 3.

Father God, You are our safe shelter and refuge; You are our strong tower. I thank You because it is only in You that the safety of my family is guaranteed. I commit the security and safety of all my family members into Your Hands. I declare that in our going out and coming in, we are safe in You. Your Word says, 'the Name of the Lord is a strong tower the righteous runs into it, and they are safe.' I declare that this is our testimony in Jesus' Name. Amen.

Further Reading: Psalm 91: 1 – 2.

213. PRAY FOR PROTECTION

Bible Passage

"You are my hiding place; you will protect me from trouble and surround me with songs of deliverance." Psalm 23: 7.

Heavenly Father, I thank You because You are my hiding place; You always protect me from trouble and surround me with songs of deliverance. I am so grateful because You are my refuge and strength, my ever-present help in times of trouble. I declare that I am protected in my going out and in my coming in. The Word of the Lord is my light, and I will not dash my foot against any stone of the enemy in Jesus' Name. Amen.

Further Reading: Psalm 46: 1.

214. PRAY FOR THE LOVE OF GOD TO GROW AND OVERWHELM EVERYONE IN YOUR FAMILY

Bible Passage

"How good and pleasant it is when God's people live together in unity" Psalm 133: 1.

Blessed Father, I thank You for Your love that we have in my family. I pray that it increases and overwhelms everyone in my family by the power of the Holy Spirit. I declare that whatever the situation, we will be bound together to go through the challenge. Nothing or situation shall be able to separate us or cause us to forsake the will of God for our lives. The Name of the Lord Jesus Christ is glorified in my family every day. Amen.

Further Reading: Romans 12: 9.

215. PRAY FOR THE SALVATION OF YOUR FAMILY MEMBERS THAT ARE NOT SAVED YET

Bible Passage

"Sirs, what must I do to be saved?" So they said, "Believe on the Lord Jesus Christ, and you will be saved, you and your household" Acts 16: 30 – 31.

The Lord Jesus said, 'except a man is born again, he cannot see the Kingdom of God.' Lord God, I pray for every member of my family that is not yet born again or received the Lord Jesus into their heart. I pray that the light of the glorious Gospel shines into their hearts and gladly receive salvation and be saved. I pray that the Holy Spirit convicts them and causes them to willingly give their hearts to the Lord in Jesus' Name. Amen.

Further Reading: Ephesians 2: 8 – 9.

216. PRAY FOR UNITY AMONG YOUR FAMILY

Bible Passage

"*Make every effort to keep the unity of the Spirit through the bond of peace*" Ephesians 4: 3.

Heavenly Father, I thank You because no matter the differences amongst my family members, the bond of unity that comes with the Gospel will unite everyone. Yes, differences are expected, but I declare that my family will not be torn apart in the Name of the Lord Jesus Christ. We will see through the difference to be united, especially for the purpose of fostering our faith in God. We are all committed to keeping the unity of the Spirit through the bond of peace in the Name of Jesus Christ. Amen.

Further Reading: Colossians 3: 14.

217. LIKE JOSHUA, DECLARE THAT YOU AND YOUR FAMILY WILL SERVE THE LORD

Bible Passage

"And if it seem evil unto you to serve the LORD, choose you this day whom ye will serve; whether the gods which your fathers served that were on the other side of the flood, or the gods of the Amorites, in whose land ye dwell: but as for me and my house, we will serve the LORD" Joshua 24: 15.

Glorious Father, in the Name of the Lord Jesus Christ, I declare that my household and I will serve the Lord. No matter the pressures and changes we see in our world today, I declare that the Lord will be our God, and He alone we will serve. I pray that we are all focused; none of us will be distracted or lured by the lust of this world to forsake our God. We are living the Christian life, and our testimonies are drawing many to serve God with us. Glory to God! Amen.

Further Reading: 1 Kings 18: 21.

218. PRAY FOR MORE GRACE FOR YOUR FAMILY MEMBERS TO EXCEL IN ALL THEY DO

Bible Passage

"He has filled them with skill to do every sort of work done by an engraver or by a designer or by an embroiderer in blue and purple and scarlet yarns and fine twined linen, or by a weaver—by any sort of workman or skilled designer" Exodus 35: 35.

Blessed Father, I thank You because of the grace we currently enjoy in our family. We are all doing great and excellent in our endeavors. I praise You for this, in Jesus' Name. Lord God, I praise for more grace to distinguish ourselves in our various careers. Your Word says that You give more grace. I ask for more grace for academics, businesses, careers, jobs, etc. I declare that our work and skills will bring us to the limelight. The world will know the truth that we have been graced in Jesus' Name. Amen.

Further Reading: Ephesians 4: 28.

219. DECLARE THAT YOUR FAMILY IS BLESSED AND PROSPEROUS

Bible Passage

"The Lord will make you abound in prosperity, in the offspring of your body and in the offspring of your beast and in the produce of your ground, in the land which the Lord swore to your fathers to give you" Deuteronomy 28: 11.

Father, I thank You for blessing my family with so many substances and prosperity. I declare that by the Holy Spirit, we are all walking in the light of this blessing in Jesus' Name. Those we know and do not even know are seeking us out to be a blessing to us. In the Name of Jesus Christ, I declare that our lips are filled with testimonies and songs of praise to God. Glory be to Your Holy Name, precious Father. Halleluiah!

Further Reading: Psalm 118: 25.

220. PRAY FOR GOD'S DIVINE HEALTH FOR YOUR FAMILY MEMBERS

Bible Passage

"Dear friend, I pray that you may enjoy good health and that all may go well with you, even as your soul is getting along well" 3 John 1: 2.

Father, I thank You for the divine health I currently enjoy in Christ. I pray that it extends to all my family members in Jesus' Name. I pray for instant healing for those that are sick of any sickness. I declare them healed from the crown of their heads to the souls of their feet. The Name of the Lord Jesus is named upon them, and they enjoy sound health in their bodies. That same Spirit that raised Jesus from the dead revitalizes their mortal bodies and causes them to stay healthy in Jesus' Name Amen.

Further Reading: Jeremiah 33: 6.

221. PRAY THAT GOD WILL RAISE MINISTERS FROM YOUR FAMILY

Bible Passage

"Before I formed you in the womb I knew you, and before you were born I set you apart and appointed you as a prophet to the nations." Jeremiah 1: 5.

Lord God, I thank You for calling us with a holy calling. I pray that You graciously raise end-time ministers from my family. It is a great privilege to serve in the Lord's vineyard. I pray that members of my family also enjoy this privilege. I declare that as many as are ready to be used by God are anointed by the Holy Spirit to become the ministers of our God. I thank You, precious Father, for this great privilege in Jesus' Name. Amen.

Further Reading: Galatians 1: 15.

222. PRAY THAT YOUR FAMILY IS SANCTIFIED: RIGHTEOUSNESS REIGNS IN YOUR FAMILY

Bible Passage

"Whoever pursues righteousness and love finds life, prosperity and honor" Proverbs 21: 21.

Blessed Father, I thank You because Your Word says that he who follows righteousness and mercy finds life, righteousness, and honor. I pray that the righteousness of God reigns in my family. There is no room for evil in my family; we are born of God. We are the righteousness of God in Christ Jesus, and we produce the fruits of righteousness. We are sanctified, holy, and we do the works of righteousness because we have been made righteous in Christ Jesus. Halleluiah!

Further Reading: Matthew 6: 33.

Chapter 10: PRAYER TO ENJOY YOUR INHERITANCE IN CHRIST

Glory to God! There is so much that the Lord God has blessed us with in Christ Jesus. He has blessed us with all that pertains to life and godliness. In Christ, we have the inheritance of eternal life, the Holy Spirit to dwell in us, God's nature of righteousness, prosperity, divine health and adoption of sonship with the Father. Also, in Christ, we have peace, unspeakable joy full of glory, grace, wisdom, God's ability, and so much more. Now that you are born again and in Christ, there is nothing that you need to enjoy your life that God has not granted you.

As you study God's Word and pray, especially the prayers contained in this category, the Spirit of God will open your eyes to see them. Yes, as you pray, your spirit will be emboldened to receive, accept and be able to appropriate them into your life. It is like receiving a Christmas present, but after a year or two, you fail to open the package to know what you were given and to start using and enjoying it. You must know your inheritance in Christ and learn to appropriate and enjoy it. That is when it becomes a blessing to you.

By the Spirit of God, as you start praying these prayers, God will cause you to become aware of all your inheritances in Christ. He will cause your spirit to receive faith to accept and start enjoying every one of them to the glory of God.

223. PRAYER FOR ACCESS INTO YOUR INHERITANCE IN CHRIST

Bible Passage

"*Giving thanks to the Father, who has qualified us to share in the inheritance of the saints in Light*" Colossians 1: 12.

Precious Father, I thank You for counting me worthy to share in the inheritance of the saints in light. I thank You for salvation and all that is in the package for me. I thank You for divine health, peace, joy, prosperity, love, wisdom, grace, glory, beauty and the ability to study and understand Your Word. Lord, thank You for granting me Your nature of righteousness, eternal life and the Holy Spirit in Jesus' Name. Amen.

Further Reading: Romans 8: 17.

224. PRAY THAT BY THE SPIRIT OF GOD AT WORK IN YOU, YOU WILL ENJOY ALL YOUR INHERITANCE IN CHRIST

Bible Passage

"And if children, heirs also, heirs of God and fellow heirs with Christ, if indeed we suffer with Him so that we may also be glorified with Him" Romans 8:17.

Father, in the Name of Jesus Christ, I pray that by the Holy Spirit who is at work in my members, I enjoy all my inheritance in Christ Jesus. Eternal life, divine health, peace, prosperity, salvation, righteousness, wisdom, faith, hope, the Holy Spirit, etc., are some of my inheritances in Christ Jesus. I declare that I am enjoying every one of them to the glory of God. The wealth of the heathen is mine. The bread and wine of Jacob are mine, the blessings of Abraham are mine. Blessed be God! Amen.

Further Reading: Acts 20: 32.

225. DECLARE THAT AS YOU STUDY THE WORD OF GOD, YOU CAN IDENTIFY ALL YOUR INHERITANCE IN CHRIST

Bible Passage

"To obtain an inheritance which is imperishable and undefiled and will not fade away, reserved in heaven for you" 1 Peter 1: 4.

I thank You, Father, for the ability to study the Word to find my inheritance therein. The entrance of Your Word illuminates; it gives direction and enlightenment. Your Word is able to deliver to me my inheritance among those that are sanctified. I pray that as I study more of Your Word, I will discover my inheritances and learn to enjoy them because they are my birthright in Christ. I declare that I have inheritances that are imperishable and undefiled and will not fade away, reserved for me here on earth and in heaven in Jesus' Name. Amen.

Further Reading: Psalm 47: 4.

226. DECLARE THAT YOU ENJOY ALL THE BLESSINGS OF SALVATION

Bible Passage

"Yet to all who received him, to those who believed in his name, he gave the right to become children of God" John 1: 12.

Glorious Father, in the Name of the Lord Jesus Christ, I thank You for the privilege of salvation in Christ Jesus. I declare that I am enjoying all the blessings of my salvation package. I am living and enjoying divine health, peace, joy, prosperity, eternal life, etc. I have given my heart to the Lord Jesus; my salvation is sure and secured. The benefits of being saved are evident in my life to the glory of God. Amen.

Further Reading: Colossians 1: 13.

227. DECLARE THAT THE WEALTH OF THE HEATHEN ARE TRANSFERRED TO YOU

Bible Passage

"But you shall be named the priests of the LORD, They shall call you the servants of our God. You shall eat the riches of the gentiles, and in their glory you shall boast" Isaiah 61: 6.

I am a child of God, the child of the Monarch of the universe. I declare that the riches and wealth of the heathen are mine. I eat the riches of the gentiles, and in their glory, I boast. They are aliens and thus cut off from God. Therefore, I inherit their wealth; their possessions are transferred to me. They are meant to gather, and as they do, their possessions become mine in the Name of Jesus. Amen.

Further Reading: Isaiah 23: 18.

228. DECLARE THAT THE BLESSING OF GOD THAT MAKE YOU RICH WITHOUT SORROWS ARE YOURS

Bible Passage

"The blessing of the LORD makes rich, and he adds no sorrow with it" Proverbs 10: 22.

Father, I thank You because Your blessing makes one rich and adds no sorrow with it. I am enjoying Your blessing as it translates to wealth, sound health, safety, hope, peace, joy, etc. I refuse all contrabands, things that are not included in the blessing of God for me. I refuse sickness, death, depression and frustration because they bring sorrow and are not part of God's blessing. I prosper in all that I do because I have the blessing of God in my life in Jesus' Name. Amen.

Further Reading: Genesis 26: 12 – 13.

229. DECLARE THAT YOUR FAITH IS ACTIVATED TO ENJOY BOTH THE SPIRITUAL AND PHYSICAL BLESSINGS THAT GOD HAS BLESSED YOU WITH

Bible Passage

"Praise be to the God and Father of our Lord Jesus Christ, who has blessed us in the heavenly realms with every spiritual blessing in Christ" Ephesians 1: 3.

Glory to God! I declare that my faith is 100 percent activated to enjoy both the spiritual and physical blessings that God has blessed me with in Christ. There is no blessing I am leaving behind; I receive all of them, and I enjoy them to the fullest. My faith is active enough to receive the blessings, no matter how big or too good they seem. I am a child of God, and I deserve the best in Jesus' Name. Amen.

Further Reading: Psalm 20: 4.

230. DECLARE THAT THE GLORIOUS THINGS THAT HAVE BEEN SPOKEN OF YOU ARE MANIFESTING IN YOUR LIFE

Bible Passage

"Glorious things are spoken of you, O city of God" Psalm 87: 3.

Praise God, Halleluiah! Father, Your Word declares that glorious things are spoken of me and that I am a city of God. Lord, I thank You for this honor in Jesus' Name. I am the light of the world, a city on the hilltop that cannot be hidden. I am the righteousness of God in Christ Jesus. Halleluiah! I am a chosen generation, a royal priesthood, a holy nation, a peculiar people set apart to show forth the praises of God. I am the salt of the earth – I preserve my world in Jesus' Name. Amen.

Further Reading: Isaiah 60: 1.

231. PRAY THAT YOU WILL ALWAYS WALK IN SUPERNATURAL FAVOR

Bible Passage

"For it is You who blesses the righteous man, O Lord, You surround him with favor as with a shield" Psalm 5: 12.

Father, in the Name of the Lord Jesus, I pray that I always walk in supernatural favor. I am favored by God and man alike. The favor of God attracts financial and material blessings to me. It causes men to seek me out to do me good. I am distinguished for honor and rare privileges because I am supernaturally favored. I enjoy unusual grace because the Lord has anointed me with great favor. By the power of the Holy Spirit, the favor of God reflects in all that I do. Amen.

Further Reading: Proverbs 3: 4.

232. DECLARE THAT NOTHING WILL ROB YOU OF YOUR INHERITANCE IN CHRIST

Bible Passage

"I will prevent pests from devouring your crops, and the vines in your fields will not drop their fruit before it is ripe," says the LORD Almighty" Malachi 3: 11.

In the Name of the Lord Jesus, I declare that nothing will rob me of my inheritance. Sin cannot cause me not to have or enjoy what the Lord has blessed me with. I declare fear and doubts have no place in my heart; thus, they cannot rob me of my inheritances. I declare that I am a doer of the Word of God and not just a hearer only. I am not ignorant of the blessings of God for me; as I study and meditate on the Word, I receive faith to enjoy my inheritance. Blessed be God forevermore! Amen.

Further Reading: Joel 2: 25.

233. DECLARE THAT THE REALITY OF YOUR JOINT-'HEIR-SHIP' WITH CHRIST WILL KEEP MANIFESTING AS YOU GROW IN CHRIST

Bible Passage

"And if you belong to Christ, then you are Abraham's seed and heirs according to the promise" Galatians 3: 29.

The Word of God declares that I am an heir of God, a joint heir with Christ Jesus. I declare that by the power of the Holy Spirit, the realities of these truths are manifested in life in Jesus' Name. Amen. As heir of God, I have been bequeathed honor, eternal life, righteousness, which is the nature of God. The Holy Spirit lives in me today because the Lord Jesus qualified me to receive Him as my helper. I function in God's grace, glory, wisdom and abilities; I have the authority to use the Name of Jesus all because I am enjoying my inheritance. Glory to God!

Further Reading: Galatians 4: 7.

Chapter 11: PRAYER FOR YOUR NATION

Do you know that if you do not pray for your nation, things will go very wrong, and you would be adversely affected? Sure, it is your responsibility to pray for your nation as if it only depends on you. The Word of God lets us know that like a roaring lion, the Devil goes about seeking whom he may devour. He uses unreasonable and wicked folks and his demons to influence wickedness all around the world. He is the one that causes outbreaks of diseases, earthquakes, rape, murder, wrong economic policies, inflations, economic meltdown, divorces in marriage, terrorist attacks, etc.

As a born again Christian, you are the right candidate to pray to restrain the Devil and his cohorts from running rampant in your nation. That is why the Spirit of God made these prayers available to you to pray for your nation. When you study your Bible, you will discover how so many stood in the gap for their nations in prayers, and God came to the rescue of those nations, especially Israel.

Now you have the opportunity to pray for the security, salvation and righteousness of folks in your country, prosperity, the wisdom of the leaders and economic improvement. Again, if you don't pray, you will not be able to even practice your Christianity. The Devil will inspire the parliament to make laws that are evil and put the citizens in bondage. However, as you pray, there will be a reassignment of demons with angels. There will be so much prosperity in the land, and you will enjoy it.

234. PRAY FOR SAFETY AND SECURITY IN YOUR COUNTRY

Bible Passage

"Except the LORD build the house, they labor in vain that build it: except the LORD keep the city, the watchman wakes but in vain" Psalm 127: 1.

Dear Lord God, I thank You for my nation. Your Word says, 'except You build a house they labor in vain that build it: except the LORD keep the city, the watchman wakes but in vain.' Father, I thank You for the safety and security of my nation. I pray that You grant our security agencies the wisdom to secure our nation. I declare that they deal wisely; they know what to do to keep our nation safe in Jesus' Name. Amen.

Further Reading: Psalm 121: 3 – 4.

235. PRAY AGAINST TERRORIST ATTACKS AGAINST YOUR NATION

Bible Passage

"There are six things that the Lord *hates, seven that are an abomination to him: haughty eyes, a lying tongue, and hands that shed innocent blood, a heart that devises wicked plans, feet that make haste to run to evil, a false witness who breathes out lies, and one who sows discord among brothers"* Proverbs 6: 16 – 19.

Father God, I thank You for the safety of my nation. I pray against any form of terrorist attack on our nation in Jesus' Name. I declare that their plans to attack my nation are scattered. However they gather or plan their wickedness, their hearts fail them. I bring all their plans to naught by the power of the Holy Spirit. I declare that before they execute their evil plans, they are caught and brought to book in Jesus' Name. Amen.

Further Reading: Psalm 34: 14.

236. PRAY THAT RIGHTEOUSNESS WILL EXALT YOUR NATION

Bible Passage

"*Righteousness exalts a nation, but sin condemns any people*" Proverbs 14: 34.

Righteous Father, I pray that my nation is exalted in righteousness. I pray that every aspect of our national life is filled with righteousness. The Word of God says, when the righteous rule, the people rejoice. I want my nation to be filled with rejoicing. Therefore, I declare that the people in our government rule with the fear of God and righteousness. Any policies that are detrimental to our economic progress and development boldly reject them in Jesus' Name. Amen.

Further Reading: Psalm 107: 34.

237. DECLARE THAT BY THE SPIRIT OF GOD, YOU WILL REAP THE FRUIT OF YOUR NATION

Bible Passage

"If you are willing and obedient, you will eat the good things of the land" Isaiah 1: 19.

Blessed Father, I thank You because the good of my nation is for me. I have sown into this country through prayers and other means. Therefore, I declare that I enjoy peace, progress, prosperity, security and abundance of blessings. In the Name of Jesus Christ, my businesses are flourishing; I am making progress and profits. Where I sow one, I get five; where I sow five, I get a hundred by the Spirit of God. I am enjoying the wealth of my nation in Jesus' Name. Amen.

Further Reading: Isaiah 25: 6.

238. PRAY FOR THE LEADERS OF YOUR NATION: DECLARE THAT THEY LEAD BY THE WISDOM OF GOD

Bible Passage

"I urge, then, first of all, that petitions, prayers, intercession and thanksgiving be made for all people—For kings, and for all that are in authority; that we may lead a quiet and peaceable life in all godliness and honesty" 1 Timothy 2: 1 – 2.

Father, I pray especially for the leaders of my nation. I pray that from the local to national levels, all the leaders, no matter their capacities, lead by the wisdom of God. I pray that the Holy Spirit will function in their hearts and cause them to always favor the policies that would enhance our national development. I declare that our leaders are bold to resist evil influences. The Christians among them are bold to make known their faith in Jesus' Name. Amen.

Further Reading: Jeremiah 29: 7.

239. PROPHECY, PROSPERITY AND BLESSINGS ON YOUR NATION

Bible Passage

"For I command you today to love the Lord your God, to walk in obedience to him, and to keep his commands, decrees and laws; then you will live and increase, and the Lord your God will bless you in the land you are entering to possess" Deuteronomy 30: 16.

Father God, in the Name of the Lord Jesus Christ, I prophecy increased prosperity and blessings on my nation. I declare that there is increased job creation for the unemployed. I pray for increased production and favorable markets for producers. I declare that our government turns out good policies that will enhance wealth creation. I prophesy God's blessings on the tourism, hospitality, agricultural, manufacturing and other services providing sectors; they are developing, flourishing and prospering by the power of the Holy Spirit. Amen.

Further Reading: Exodus 23: 25.

240. REBUKE THE SPIRIT OF WICKEDNESS IN YOUR NATION

Bible Passage

"Woe to those who scheme iniquity, who work out evil on their beds! When morning comes, they do it, for it is in the power of their hands" Micah 2: 1.

In the Name of the Lord Jesus Christ, I rebuke the activities of the evil through individuals, groups or circumstances to destabilize our nation. I pray that all their efforts are brought to naught by the power of the Holy Spirit. I declare that wicked activities are weakened. The perpetrators are giving their hearts to the Lord Jesus. The hearts of the youths are disabused from engaging in wickedness. I pull down the spirit of violence in our nation by the power of the Holy Spirit. Halleluiah!

Further Reading: Isaiah 3: 11.

241. PRAY THAT EVERY HINDRANCE TO THE SPREAD OF THE GOSPEL IN YOUR NATION IS DISMANTLED

Bible Passage

"Finally, brethren, pray for us, that the word of the Lord may have free course, and be glorified, even as it is with you" 2 Thessalonians 3: 1.

I thank You, precious Father, for the spread of the Gospel in my nation. I declare that every home and family receive the Gospel gladly in Jesus' Name. I pull down every hindrance to the Gospel reaching the hearts of men. By the power in the Name of Jesus Christ, I declare such forces and influences quashed. Their courage and influences are failing them. No matter how powerful they are, the Name of the Lord Jesus is high and more powerful. They fail in their enterprises to frustrate the Gospel in the Name of Jesus. Amen.

Further Reading: Acts 19: 20.

242. PRAY FOR INCREASED ACTIVITIES OF SALVATION ANGELS: STIRRING MANY TO RECEIVE CHRIST IN YOUR NATION

Bible Passage

"Cornelius stared at him in fear and asked, "What is it, Lord?" The angel answered, "Your prayers and gifts to the poor have ascended as a memorial offering before God...Now send men to Joppa to bring back a man named Simon who is called Peter" Acts 10: 4 – 5.

Father, I thank You for the increased activities of salvation angels in my nation. The hearts of many are being stirred to receive Jesus Christ into their hearts as Lord and Savior. Your Word says Your power to save souls is in the preaching of the Gospel. I pray that as the Gospel is reaching every corner of this nation, men, women, boys and girls are gladly receiving salvation in Jesus' Name. They are responding to alter calls by the power of the Holy Spirit. Glory to God! Amen.

Further Reading: Psalm 107: 14.

243. PRAY FOR YOUR NATION: DECLARE THAT EVERY SECTOR OF YOUR NATIONAL LIFE IS FRUITFUL

Bible Passage

"In a very short time, will not Lebanon be turned into a fertile field and the fertile field seems like a forest?" Isaiah 29: 17.

I declare that there is fruitfulness in our land. Our soils are fertile for agricultural production. The Holy Spirit is opening our eyes to see the good in our land; we are discovering natural resources of commercial quantity. Our economy is booming, and investors from far and near are coming to our nation to create wealth and prosperity by the power of the Holy Spirit. In the Name of Jesus Christ, I declare that life is not difficult in our nation; the cost of living is cheap. Amen.

Further Reading: Psalm 107:35.

244. PRAY FOR YOUR NATION'S ECONOMY

Bible Passage

"I will bless those who bless you and him who dishonors you I will curse, and in you all the families of the earth shall be blessed" Genesis 12: 3.

Heavenly Father, I thank You for saving our nation and its economy from total ruin as a result of the effects of Covid-19. Lord, I pray for a total recovery for any aspect that was adversely affected. I pray for growth and new opportunities in our economy, opportunities that would enhance the standard of living of the populace. I thank You for new employment opportunities for those who lose their jobs in Jesus' Name. Amen.

Further Reading: Proverbs 21: 20.

Chapter 12: PRAYER FOR GOD'S GRACE

The Word of God says it is not by power, not by might but by the Spirit of the Lord. This is grace; when you achieve your goals effortlessly, without struggles. Remember that the blessings of God make you rich and add no sorrow with it. Grace is when men and women and circumstances fall upon themselves to do you good. Grace is when you put in one, you reap five, and when you put in five, you receive a hundred, and when you put in a hundred, you harvest millions. Glory to God!

The grace of God lifts; it takes you to heights you never thought possible, even when you are not qualified for it. It singles you out for favor, honor, privileges and opportunities. It brings you out and sets you in stardom; you become a beauty and wonder to your world.

As you pray in this session, expect to receive more grace and sudden favor from men and women. Your ministry will take a new turn, moving upward and forward because you would have been so graced. Grace will cause your errors to be minimized because it is God that is at work in you now. The prayers here will launch you into a level where you will enjoy things you've never worked for. The Spirit of God will help you do things, and where others struggle, you will find grace; you will receive special abilities. Your path in life will become straight and smooth because of these prayers.

245. PRAY FOR MORE GRACE

Bible Passage

"But as you excel in everything—in faith, in speech, in knowledge, in all earnestness, and in our love for you—see that you excel in this act of grace also" 2 Corinthians 8: 7.

Father, I thank You for Your increased grace upon my life. I am graced in every area of my life; I am graced with Your glory, beauty, ability, excellence and Your divine presence. There is nothing I cannot achieve because the grace of God is daily multiplied in my life. Thus, I excel in everything. I declare that as I study more of the Word, the grace of God increased in me more and more. I win every day by the grace of God at work in me in Jesus' Name. Amen.

Further Reading: Ephesians 4: 7.

246. PRAY FOR MORE OF GOD'S GRACE TO FULFILL YOUR DESTINY

Bible Passage

"And the God of all grace, who called you to his eternal glory in Christ, after you have suffered a little while, will himself restore you and make you strong, firm and steadfast" 1 Peter 5: 10.

Blessed Father, I thank You because You are the God of all grace who called me to Your eternal glory in Christ Jesus. I declare that I am growing in grace more and more to function in life. In all that I do, I refuse to struggle; I do not stress but function in grace to achieve all. I function by the leading of the Holy Spirit in all that I do. The men and recourses to get things done are always available to me in Jesus' Name. Amen.

Further Reading: 1 Corinthians 1: 9.

247. PRAY THAT THE GRACE OF GOD CAUSES MEN FROM FAR AND NEAR TO FAVOR YOU

Bible Passage

"The Lord bless you and keep you; the Lord make his face shine on you and be gracious to you; the Lord turn his face toward you and give you peace" Numbers 6: 24 – 26.

Father, Your Word says that men travelled from distant lands and clans to see Solomon, and they came with great wealth to honor him. I declare that from far and near, men are seeking me out to favor me because I am born again and function by Your grace. I pray that in the Name of Jesus, nothing shall be said to be too good for me. Nothing is difficult for me to achieve because I am so graced. I thank You, Father, in Jesus' Name. Amen.

Further Reading: Deuteronomy 28:

248. DECLARE THAT YOU HAVE MORE GRACE FOR MINISTRY

Bible Passage

"The faith and love that spring from the hope stored up for you in heaven and about which you have already heard in the true message of the gospel that has come to you. In the same way, the gospel is bearing fruit and growing throughout the whole world – just as it has been doing among you since the day you heard it and truly understood God's grace" Colossians 1: 5-6.

These are the lasts days; I pray, Father, for more grace to function and excel in ministry. Your Word says we have been called into the ministry of reconciliations. Thus, I declare that I am more than ever so committed to reaching my world for the Lord Jesus Christ. In service to the Lord, I pray for more grace to serve as I should so that, at the end, I will not be cast away. I declare that I recognize opportunities for service in Jesus' Name. Amen.

Further Reading: Romans 10: 18.

249. DECLARE THAT YOU HAVE RECEIVED FORGIVENESS OF SINS THROUGH GOD'S GRACE

Bible Passage

"In him we have redemption through his blood, the forgiveness of sins, in accordance with the riches of God's grace" Ephesians 1: 7.

I thank You, Father, because, in the Lord Jesus Christ, I have redemption through His blood, the forgiveness of sins, in accordance with the riches of Your grace. I declare that I do not feel condemnation or a sense of guilt because the Father has graciously lavished His grace on me. I am loved by God; hence, I cannot feel inferior or condemned. Nothing can ever cause me to walk in unrighteousness because that is not the place the Father has placed in Him. Halleluiah! Amen.

Further Reading: Acts 2: 28.

250. I DECLARE THAT THE GRACE OF GOD IS SUFFICIENT FOR ANYTHING I WANT TO DO OR ACHIEVE IN LIFE

Bible Passage

"But he said to me, "My grace is sufficient for you, for my power is made perfect in weakness." Therefore I will boast all the more gladly of my weaknesses, so that the power of Christ may rest upon me" 2 Corinthians 12: 9.

Father, I thank You so much because Your grace is sufficient for me in whatever I want to do or achieve. Precious Lord, Your power is made perfect in my weaknesses; You are my sufficiency, ability, wisdom, and strength. I declare that in my inadequacies, You are my help, my energy and speed to continue and to excel. I declare that the power of Christ rests upon me to do and achieve my goals. Glory to God! Amen.

Further Reading: 1 Corinthians 2: 5.

SELVA SUGUNENDRAN

ALL BOOKS PUBLISHED BY AUTHOR OF THIS BOOK

BOOKS ON CREATION & EVOLUTION

SELVA SUGUNENDRAN

BOOKS ON WELLNESS & HEALTH

10

11

12

13

14

BOOKS ON ALZHEIMER'S & DEMENTIA

SELVA SUGUNENDRAN

BOOKS ON SUCCESS

BOOK ON AUTISM & ASPERGER'S SYNDROME

SELVA SUGUNENDRAN

BOOKS ON CHRISTIAN BELIEFS: FAITH, PRAYER, MIRACLES